BOLD
Dr. Leon van Rooyen

"Bold Christians will turn this world right side up!

ISBN 978-1-940725-88-8

Published by Dr. Leon van Rooyen
PO Box 47599
Tampa, FL 33646
USA

Dedication

I dedicate this book to Faith Broadcasting Family of Networks, based out of my hometown East London, South Africa. Faith Broadcast Network is a family of premier Christian television channels bringing the Gospel of Jesus Christ to homes on the continent of Africa and beyond. In my opinion, Faith Broadcast Network epitomizes the potential of communicating the Gospel, Bible Teaching, and family entertainment. I applaud the bold vision and passion of Andre and Jenny Roebert and their entire Team.

Dr. Andre Roebert

I want to thank my dear friend, Dr. Andre Roebert, President of River Group of Companies and Faith Broadcasting Family of Networks, for his Foreword. I smiled when I read his gracious words about my being bold. Andre is the boldest leader I know. I have seen him make decisions that are so momentous, and he appears to be unfazed by the enormity of what he has done. As a result of the decisions he makes, his ministry and leadership impact the Continent of Africa and many nations beyond. I admire my friend for his boldness and strength of character and am grateful for my relationship with him, his family and the Team at Faith Broadcast Family of Networks.

Contents

Foreword   i

Introduction   v

Chapter 1 – Bold Approach to God   1

Chapter 2 – Bold Prayers   15

Chapter 3 – Bold Faith   37

Chapter 4 – Bold Witness   51

Chapter 5 – Bold in the Spirit   67

Chapter 6 – Bold in the Face of Persecution   85

Chapter 7 – Bold in Spiritual Warfare   105

Chapter 8 – Bold Giving   127

Chapter 9 – Bold Leaders   143

Foreword

...The enemy of the church and our souls wants us to live ordinary lives. He doesn't mind if we have a form of godliness as long as the genuine power of God can't flow through our lives. He doesn't mind if we are a part of a Christian audience, but he will do everything possible to prevent us from doing the will of God. He is terrified of Christians who are equipped, empowered, and mobilized....

"To be bold means to be courageous, confident, or fearless. A bold person is willing to take risks. Boldness to approach and receive from God because of our state of righteousness in Christ Jesus." These profound statements are a direct quote from Dr. Leon van Rooyen's book 'Bold,' and truer words have not been spoken.

Living bold is not a quality demonstrated in the moments where our lives are going well, and we experience those mountain top moments. Rather, it's what comes from the relentless faith and tenacious steadfastness we develop in trusting God and His Word while trudging through the valleys of uncertainty and shadows of hopelessness. Living boldly is when you make a choice to cross over from the natural way of living to the supernatural. It's really an 'all or nothing way of life'.

As you journey through his book, Dr. Leon shows from Scripture, how people who demonstrated this boldness of faith, appeared courageous and fearless, not from a confidence that resulted from their own abilities or attributes, but rather from a complete trust and dependence in the One they served and worshiped. A courageous believer develops a relationship with God that is tested and tried through extreme challenges. It's where a bold act of obedience balances on the risk of losing every ounce of earthly reputation or gaining eternal significance for the Kingdom of God. A risk well worth the journey, but one few are willing to take.

For my wife and I, the past twenty-five years of ministry have proven this to be our reality. To make a significant difference in this world, walking in boldness is an essential trait for every believer to master in their journey of faith. In this timely book, Dr. Leon van Rooyen covers many aspects of living boldly. It will take you on a journey from where you are today, to where you need to be - living strong in the Word of God.

Over the many years of personally knowing Dr. Leon, my wife and I have witnessed how this 'bold' way of life he writes about, is characteristic of his own. His passion and fearless courage to preach and demonstrate the Gospel of Jesus Christ over all these years has been a tremendous inspiration to us and many others. As a young man, Dr. Leon received a word from God that he chose to believe, forsake all else and follow the call. This took him on a life long journey to nations all over the world, fulfilling his God-given mandate. As our friendship has grown stronger over the years, we have truly seen his bold approach towards his faith, his prayer life, and his witness to nonbelievers abound.

Being bold in the Spirit must be a way of life, which is exactly what gives Dr. Leon the credibility to write on the subject. He has personally demonstrated this boldness of faith, especially in the face of some of the greatest persecutions life could throw at him. He is one of the boldest leaders and givers to the work of Christ we have the privilege of knowing. In this book, you will discover that life is a journey to success, and every step needs to be taken with boldness. I trust that you will enjoy it as much as we have. But more than just enjoying it, you will study its truth and grow from its practical wisdom as you apply it to every area of life. May your days of feeling faint and battle weary be something of the past as your strength and courage are renewed by the truth found on the pages of this book.

Be blessed with this must read!

Dr. Andre Roebert
River Group of Companies
Faith Broadcasting Family of Networks

Introduction

"The wicked flee when no one pursues, But the righteous are bold as a lion" (Proverbs 28:1).

Lions are bold animals; they rule enormous swathes of land, and they move around their domain with dignity and courage. As the righteous, we are likened to bold lions, and we must take dominion. In other words, keep our territory for the glory of God. Jesus, the Lion of the tribe of Judah, exhibited this boldness throughout His ministry. The courage seen in the Lord as He faced opposition, criticism and ultimately His death inspires us.

"But one of the elders said to me, 'Do not weep. Behold, the Lion of the tribe of Judah, the Root of David, has prevailed to open the scroll and to loose its seven seals'" (Revelation 5:5).

We are living in critical times; truly we are in the last of the last days. There is so much that must be accomplished to win this generation to Christ. Many nations remain in darkness and the doors of entrance to proclaim the Gospel are firmly sealed. There is growing persecution and animosity against the Church. However, we must be bold to make a stand in the face of open hostility. Regardless of the opposition we must keep pressing forward until the Gospel is preached to the ends of the earth.

The devil would love to humiliate the Church concerning our righteousness, faith and the power of God being released through our lives. As those who are called out of darkness into the marvelous light, we need every Christian to take their rightful place in their calling and ministry. We must stand shoulder-to-shoulder and boldly move as one man touching the world around our lives. We are on the winning team! I have read the back of the Book—our God wins, and He has also made us winners. We are more that conquerors! Therefore, we can be bold because the gates of hades will not prevail, the Church will be glorious, magnificent and victorious. We the Church, are going to fulfill our purpose and God's plan in our generation. It's amazing what one young man accomplished because he was bold. David won an enormous victory against the Philistines and saved the day. All his brothers, King Saul, and the army were afraid to stand up to Goliath. However, this young anointed man made a bold stance and saved a nation from defeat and humiliation. He changed the course of Israel's history. Even today in honor of his life and courage, the Star of David is on the flag of Israel. Just like David did so many thousands of years ago, as Christians, we also need to confront the giants of our era. As you read this book, it will inspire you to be bold, to be lion-hearted, and to live a large life for the glory of God. Be BOLD, be strong for the Lord your God is with you!

Dr. Leon van Rooyen

Chapter 1

Bold Approach to God

We often quote the famous scripture that says: "I can <u>do</u> all things through Christ" (Philippians 4:13). However, I have found that many Christians who quote this verse don't actually do much. Many Christians are living sterile lives that produce very little fruit. They are not engaged in ministry activities or busy about the business of eternity. Most times, fear stops them from launching out to do or say what God told them. They want Jesus to say, "Well Done!" without actually doing anything. However, an ordinary person will do extraordinary things when they are bold. Bold Christians don't just talk about what they want to accomplish but they get out and do it.

Bold people take on the impossible; they press through every barrier until what they want to accomplish becomes possible. Bold Christians will get the job done, even though it may appear to be impossible, knowing that through the ability of Christ they can do all things.

We are living in the most crucial days concerning the Church and the advancement of God's Kingdom. There is a violent war raging in the realms of darkness against a very determined enemy, whose goal is to stop the Church from fulfilling its mission, which is to reach this generation.

BOLD

Though the devil is a defeated enemy, he is nonetheless determined to mute the Gospel. The enemy of the Church and our souls wants us to live ordinary lives.

- He doesn't mind if we have a form of godliness as long as the genuine power of God can't flow through our lives.

- He doesn't mind if we are a part of a Christian audience, but he will do everything possible to prevent us from doing the will of God. He is terrified of Christians who are equipped, empowered, and mobilized.

But this is what was spoken by the prophet Joel: 'And it shall come to pass in the last days, says God, that I will pour out My Spirit upon all flesh; Your sons and your daughters shall prophesy, Your young men shall see visions, Your old men shall dream dreams. And on My menservants and on My maidservants I will pour out My Spirit in those days; And they shall prophesy. I will show wonders in heaven above and signs in the earth beneath: Blood and fire and vapor of smoke. The sun shall be turned into darkness, And the moon into blood, Before the coming of the great and awesome day of the LORD. And it shall come to pass that whoever calls on the name of the LORD shall be saved (Acts 2:16-21).

The last days began over two thousand years ago. Peter interpreted the prophetic declaration of Joel as starting to be fulfilled on the Day of Pentecost. We could say that we are now in the last of the last days or even the last seconds of the last days. If this is true, then the devil knowing that his time is short wants to prevent an anointed people from being raised up to prophesy, run with the vision, proclaim the Gospel and see the salvation of multitudes.

"Therefore, rejoice, O heavens, and you who dwell in them! Woe to the inhabitants of the earth and the sea! For the devil has come down to you, having great wrath, because he knows that he has a short time" (Revelation 12:12).

According to the prophet Joel, bold Christians will prophesy, they will run with the vision, raise up sons and daughters to prophesy and proclaim the Gospel in the face of hostility. This is our day!

Having a South African accent is a good thing—well at least sometimes. For some reason, people love my accent and so I often go into places of business, and people ask me to keep talking to them. Invariably, I start with, "For God so loved the world!" With a big smile, I say, "Do you want me to keep on talking or stop here?"

One of the disadvantages of my accent is when I use Siri on my device; she doesn't understand anything I ask. One day, I asked Siri to get me directions to the nearest Starbucks. She came back with something like, "I cannot locate a hospital with that name." I just about threw my phone out the window of my car. How did Siri get "hospital" in my request? My accent is different, but it's not that thick that it could even sound like "hospital." Sometimes, I wonder why these devices are called smartphones. They should be called stupid phones!

Back to my accent issues, recently, I was praying for the impartation of boldness for some God-hungry Christians. As I was moving down the prayer line, I got to a man who had a "deer in the headlights look" and said to me, "Please don't pray for me...I don't want to be bald! I replied, "Dude! I'm praying for the spirit of boldness, not baldness."

Define Bold:

To be bold means to be courageous, confident, or fearless. A bold person is willing to take risks. Boldness should not be confused with arrogance. The measure of your authority should not exceed the measure of humility. We may enter the presence of the thrice holy God of Isaiah 6 with boldness but not with arrogance.

A while ago, I was praying for a person who was lamenting, "I am unworthy!" This sounded like humility but in the depth of my heart, I felt an irritation. Something was wrong. I knew that the person was saying the right thing, but I also discerned that what was being said was conflicting with the Word of God. My initial thought was not one of being critical because I remembered the story when Jesus discussed the difference between the self-righteous Pharisee and the humble tax collector:

Also He spoke this parable to some who trusted in themselves that they were righteous, and despised others: "Two men went up to the temple to pray, one a Pharisee and the other a tax collector. The Pharisee stood and prayed thus with himself, 'God, I thank You that I am not like other men—extortionists, unjust, adulterers, or even as this tax collector. I fast twice a week; I give tithes of all that I possess.' And the tax collector, standing afar off, would not so much as raise his eyes to heaven, but beat his breast, saying, 'God, be merciful to me a sinner!' I tell you, this man went down to his house justified rather than the other; for everyone who exalts himself will be humbled, and he who humbles himself will be exalted (Luke 18:9-14).

I thought, perhaps, this man was humble like the tax collector. Then, it occurred to me that he was praying out with a sense of anguish believing that he had no access to God. I realized that this dear man's ignorance of the Word concerning the goodness of God would limit him from receiving what God had so richly provided for him.

The death of Jesus Christ on the cross secured for us what we could not gain through our efforts, discipline, holiness, or performances.

When we were yet sinners, Christ died for us. When He did this, He provided for us what we could not provide for ourselves. This is why salvation is the free gift of God. Jesus paid a debt for us that we could not pay for ourselves. He provided for us what we could not provide for ourselves. This is why we sing the classic old hymn "Amazing Grace!"

- Our giving could not pave a way to stand in righteousness before God; our generosity would never be sufficient.
- Our morality and purity would never be pure enough to gain us access to the throne of God.
- Our works would never be good enough to save us. Even if we labored at the Gospel and prayer, we would still fall short of the holy requirements to stand before God.

Sinners cannot access the glories of God, but the righteous can approach with confidence.

"All have sinned and come short of the glory of God" (Romans 3:23).

"There is none righteous, no, not one" (Romans 3:10).

As you can see from reading these two verses, man is in a terrible predicament because all have sinned. Without being saved from our sins, we have no access to God. However, God made a way in that He sent Jesus, who knew no sin to take our place. Jesus bore our iniquities and offers us forgiveness and a brand new beginning. "For He made Him who knew no sin to be sin for us, that we might become the righteousness of God in Him. As sinners, we cannot access the glories of God, but as saints, we have direct and uninterrupted access to God" (2 Corinthians 5:21).

"In whom we have boldness and access with confidence through faith in Him" (Ephesians 3:12).

"Therefore, brethren, having boldness to enter the Holiest by the blood of Jesus, by a new and living way which He consecrated for us, through the veil, that is, His flesh" (Hebrews 10:19-20).

"Therefore, brethren, having boldness to enter the Holiest by the blood of Jesus" (Hebrews 10:19)—an amazing truth is revealed in this verse. It is by the blood of Jesus that we have been given entrance or access to God. His blood shouts louder than our guilt, shame, failures, and sins. When our deeds say, we are unworthy, the blood of Jesus declares that we are worthy. When our works say that you cannot approach; there is not enough to give you the access code then the blood says that you can access—not just access but you can access with boldness.

Now, back to my prayer-line...

The man who was saying "I am unworthy." He was not a sinner but a saint; I knew him. He was saved or born again. He had become a new creation. I asked myself the question, was he where he should be in his walk with God? I considered that perhaps he was weak and struggling in some areas of his life. These issues would not threaten his salvation or prevent him from operating in the dominion of the name of Jesus. I instinctively knew that as a child of God, these unresolved issues would not hinder his life from being touched by the hand of God unless he got into an agreement with the devil.

Perhaps he was not feeling like a saint; he may not even have been acting like a saint. Maybe, on his way to church, he had an argument with his wife and in anger raised his voice. At that moment in prayer, he may have felt very insecure in the presence of the holiness of God. Probably the devil, (the accuser of the brethren was reminding him why he could not receive) I could hear the devil's accusations:

- You are unworthy to be healed; you must stay sick.
- You are unworthy to have your prayers answered; you have not prayed enough.
- You are unworthy to be Spirit-filled because you haven't done this, or you have done that.

Can you hear the devil's accusations? This dear brother was persuaded by the liar and found himself drawn into an agreement with the accuser. This man began to say what he had heard in his mind all night, "I am unworthy!" He heard it in the worship time; he heard it in the prayer time. He heard it when the preacher read from the Bible.

In my spirit, I could hear him making these faith debilitating statements. However, deep in my spirit I also heard another voice; it was the sound that I have grown to know the "still small voice." This was the voice that I recognized as the sound of revelation; it's the voice of agreement with the Word of God.

Only Jesus is worthy to receive praise, honor, and glory, but we are worthy to be healed, filled, and empowered by the Spirit of God.

"You are worthy, O Lord, to receive glory and honor and power; For You created all things, and by Your will they exist and were created" (Revelation 4:11).

While I knew that Jesus alone was worthy to be praised, I also recognized that by the blood of Jesus this man had been made worthy to receive from His generous nail-scarred hands.

I cried out from the depth of my being, "No! You are not unworthy to receive! You are worthy to receive! That's a lie from the pit of darkness. You are being robbed of your rights and inheritance as a co-heir together with Christ. The blood has prevailed and has made you a partaker of the divine nature.

Then I heard a loud voice saying in heaven, "Now salvation, strength, the Kingdom of our God, and the power of His Christ have come. For the accuser of our brethren, who accused them before our God day and night, has been cast down. "And they overcame him by the blood of the Lamb and by the word of their testimony, and they did not love their lives to the death" (Revelation 12:10-11).

You are worthy to be healed, filled, empowered and to do all that God has called you to do! You are not unworthy because the blood of Jesus shouts louder than your guilt and failure. Hallelujah!

Faith is required to receive from God

"But without faith it is impossible to please Him, for he who comes to God must believe that He is, and that He is a rewarder of those who diligently seek Him" (Hebrews 11:6).

- Faith is the product of the Word of God.
- Faith is confident because of the character of God.
- Faith is the product of the recreated spirit man; it is not the product of your mind or feelings. Your circumstances cannot give you confidence or boldness. Your circumstances will always be a contradiction and in opposition to the Word of God.

Our confidence to approach a holy God is established in the revelation of the righteousness of God. When we know that we can approach Him, it removes the sense of unworthiness and guilt.

"Love has been perfected among us in this: that we may have boldness in the day of judgment; because as He is, so are we in this world" (1 John 4:17).

"There is therefore now no condemnation to those who are in Christ Jesus, who do not walk according to the flesh, but according to the Spirit" (Romans 8:1).

"For He made Him who knew no sin to be sin for us, that we might become the righteousness of God in Him" (2 Corinthians 5:21).

"For God so loved the world that He gave His only begotten Son, that whoever believes in Him should not perish but have everlasting life. For God did not send His Son into the world to condemn the world, but that the world through Him might be saved" (John 3:16-17).

Just like the man who was feeling unworthy in my prayer line, there are many people in the church who struggle to receive from God because they feel unworthy. They do not understand the position they have in Christ Jesus or what it means to be saved. They live in a constant sense of unworthiness with a guilt-consciousness and they feel too ashamed to receive what God has provided. It is essential that we discover our position in Christ.

You are the righteousness of God

We are not to be arrogantly self-righteous, because we are made righteous by the blood of Jesus. We can best describe righteousness as being in right standing with God. Through righteousness, we are given the ability to approach God with confidence, without a sense of guilt, shame, or unworthiness.

BOLD

We are not saved by our personal purity but by the grace of God; this position of righteousness is in spite of our mistakes and failings. The devil is the accuser of the believers and wants us to live in a sense of unworthiness, but he is defeated. When you stand boldly against him he has no power over you. You are an overcomer!

"And they overcame him by the blood of the Lamb and by the word of their testimony, and they did not love their lives to the death" (Revelation 12:11).

In righteousness, you stand before God as a son; you stand before all men equal (male, female, rich, poor, educated or uneducated, there is no caste in Christ).

- In righteousness, you are more than a conqueror; you are far above all principalities and powers, and you are over all demons as a master.
- In righteousness, all the promises of God are yours.
- In righteousness, you are worthy to receive from God.

Unfortunately, many Christians live defeated lives because they don't grasp the place that they have in Christ. It's time to rise in your new creation identity to understand that you are not a mere man, but you are a child of the Most High. Jesus Christ has given you dominion and authority over the devil. You don't have to be defeated by Satan any longer. You are in Christ, and Christ is in you. You no longer have to be intimidated by a sin-consciousness. You are forgiven; you are righteous; you are justified by the blood of Jesus.

"Arise, shine; for thy light is come, and the glory of the Lord is risen upon thee. For, behold, the darkness shall cover the earth, and gross darkness the people: but the Lord shall arise upon thee, and his glory shall be seen upon thee" (Isaiah 60:1-2).

We need to be awakened in revelation knowledge to our true identity and access in Christ.

> Therefore I also, after I heard of your faith in the Lord Jesus and your love for all the saints, do not cease to give thanks for you, making mention of you in my prayers: that the God of our Lord Jesus Christ, the Father of glory, may give to you the spirit of wisdom and revelation in the knowledge of Him, the eyes of your understanding being enlightened; that you may know what is the hope of His calling, what are the riches of the glory of His inheritance in the saints, and what is the exceeding greatness of His power toward us who believe, according to the working of His mighty power which He worked in Christ when He raised Him from the dead and seated Him at His right hand in the heavenly places, far above all principality and power and might and dominion, and every name that is named, not only in this age but also in that which is to come. And He put all things under His feet, and gave Him to be head over all things to the

Church, which is His body, the fullness of Him who fills all in all (Ephesians 1:15-22).

Now, with boldness, you can draw near to God and live your life to the fullest. You can receive all that God has for your life. You can do all that God has required of you. Yes! You can, with boldness do all things that God has called you to do. Nothing and no one can stop you. I love what God said to Joshua; I know that He is saying this to you as well: "No man shall be able to stand before you all the days of your life; as I was with Moses, so I will be with you. I will not leave you nor forsake you" (Joshua 1:5).

Chapter 2

Bold in Prayer

Jesus Culture sings the powerful song that declares "There's an army rising up...Break every chain...There's power in the name of Jesus." This is not only a beautiful song, but it is a prophetic declaration that God's people are powerful. When we pray in the name of Jesus changes are taking place in the lives of people, homes, cities, and nations. If we don't believe that our prayers are accomplishing something, then why bother to pray? When we pray as individuals or collectively, we can move mountains and change the spiritual climatic conditions. Something happens as we pray. God moves, angels are dispatched, and demons flee their post and retreat. It is true, prayer is powerful, and it is time for Christians to pray bold prayers.

God is raising up a generation of mighty followers—young and mature lovers of Jesus. These believers are bold! They are not weak "down in the mouth," feel sorry for themselves people. They are not gutless, weak-kneed, "namby-pamby" believers! They are bold in the spirit, bold in faith, and bold in prayer.

There is a tremendous need to address the Church concerning being bold in prayer because it is my observation that many Christians spend little time in prayer. As a matter of fact, there are some Christians who are prayerless unless they face an emergency; they probably spend less than a few minutes in prayer a day.

15

BOLD

Many Christians have become prayerless because they are independent, or they trust themselves more than God. Some believers place greater confidence in people rather than in God. Furthermore, many Christians have grown up in prayerless churches and have never seen their spiritual leaders exemplifying the power of prayer. They have never received biblical training in the power of prayer.

Others have backed away from praying because they have lost faith. Perhaps, they were trusting God for a breakthrough and when they did not receive the answer, they began to doubt the provision of God. There are various reasons why people have backed away from personal and corporate prayer meetings. Regardless of the reason, the end-result is that the lives of Christians have become spiritually anemic because they have neglected to pray. For this same reason, the churches have not seen the full manifestation of God's power. Pulpits have lost the fire of God because even the preachers have become too busy to pray.

I have traveled to five continents and many countries. Along the way, I have taken the time to study various religions to see how they practice their faith. I am often provoked and challenged when I see the devotion of various religions and their ways of expressing their worship. I have entered mosques, temples and watched African tribes dance through the night paying homage to their ancestors. When I see these people pray, it stirs something in me. They pray to idols and gods that are made with their hands. They honor the writings of prophets who have come and gone and have left their devotees with a way of life and a false sense of eternity. Yet, I am blown away by the great zeal these followers display in their pursuit of spirituality. Sometimes, I am amazed at the loyalty of these religionists in comparison to the lack of commitment demonstrated by Christians to the Living God. Having visited these places of worship, and seeing their abandoned and extravagant adulation, I am often challenged by their determination and sacrifices made.

What makes Christianity different from all other religions?

Essentially the differences between Christianity and all other religions are:

1. We worship and pray to a God who hears and cares; they pray to an impersonal god who has no power to help them.

2. We have the assurance of salvation based on what Jesus has done for us by dying in our place versus our works and discipline. We are saved by grace and faith in Jesus Christ. They think they are saved by their devotion and disciplines.

3. We have bold access through grace to the immediate presence of God. They attempt to gain the attention of their gods.

4. We have a personal relationship with God as sons while they have no relationship other than identifying with their religion.

All religions pray but the difference is when believers pray, something happens. Our prayers can change the landscape by moving mountains or changing the climatic conditions. Instinctively, when we are born again, we know that we have uninterrupted access to God, and so it is as normal for us to pray as it is to breathe. In fact, it has been said that the life breath for the believer is prayer. If this is the case, then why have people who confess faith in Christ stopped praying?

Too busy! It should be said that when we are too busy to pray then we are too busy. There is no doubt that life can be a hustle. It seems that our "to do" list ever increases with daily responsibilities. Some people work long hours and when they get back home, there is still so much to accomplish. They also have to carve out time for their families, churches and recreational activities. However, regardless of how busy you are, you need to take time and set it aside to seek the Lord.

"Evening, and morning and at noon I will pray, and cry aloud, and He shall hear my voice" (Psalm 55:17).

Notice the consistency in the psalmist's prayer; he prayed evening, morning and at noon. A Christian who desires to access the power of God and who wants a strong faith will be a person of prayer.

Self-Reliant! As mentioned earlier, one of the reasons many believers have stopped praying is because they have trusted in themselves more than God. They believe that they can get themselves through life on their own abilities and resources. I am sure that deep down in their hearts, they would love to receive God's help but in their minds, this is too good to be true.

In some instances, they probably think that if they got themselves into a bad situation, they need to get themselves out of it. But God is good and His mercy endures forever. In other words, when we are in trouble or need, God doesn't help us because we deserve it; He helps us in spite of what we caused or what happened. We don't have our prayers answered because we have earned the right through our discipline or industry. The Christian who is strong and self-disciplined should still be God-dependent and the one who is weak also needs God. To be God-dependent is not a weakness, rather, it is humility. We have a good Father in heaven who is willing to help us in our needs through answering our prayers. Though we may feel unworthy to ask God to intervene in our life, the blood of Jesus makes us worthy to have our prayer petitions heard by God.

"Be anxious for nothing, but in everything by prayer and supplication, with thanksgiving, let your requests be made known to God; and the peace of God, which surpasses all understanding, will guard your hearts and minds through Christ Jesus" (Philippians 4:6-7).

The goodness and the mercy of God allow us to draw close to Him to make our requests known. The blood of Jesus makes us righteous and gives us uninterrupted access to God.

Prayer disappointment! This is a little difficult to pen because I want to be transparent with you but at the same time, I don't want to imply that God does not answer prayers. As far as I am concerned, God is good, and He answers the prayer of faith. At the same time, for various reasons, some prayers don't get answered or appear unanswered. Therefore, I have discovered that people back away from seeking God because it has left them in a place of disappointment. I could write a couple of chapters on why some prayers appear not to be answered. But if I address that subject, it would distract from the topic entitled, "Bold" and so suffice to say that God hears and answers prayers of faith.

After faith-filled prayers, friends and loved ones have died, others remain sick, and it appears as if our prayers have become a waste of time and energy. As a result, some Christians have become disillusioned. With their misguided concept that prayer is like playing a game of roulette, they mistakenly think that some days, you hit a winner and other days, you walk away having lost your money.

I need to assure you that prayer is not like gambling. People who gamble, win some and probably lose a lot more than they win. When you pray, you don't have to hit the jackpot to have your prayers answered. God doesn't have bad hair days where He is disconnected and easily irritated by the cries of His people. God is good! He is always good; God will never be evil. He is good all the time and there will never be a time when He is not good. He answers the prayer of faith. I would choose to stand on the promises of the Word of God than on any other foundation. I have said this before, and I will say it again—even if I was so ill that I was on oxygen, confined to a wheelchair and there was no natural help available from the medical specialists, I would still confess Jesus as my healer. The condition of my body and my experiences are not the final authority. The final authority is the Word of God and I will preach that God answers prayer and heals the sick to my dying breath. My confession will always be this hymn of faith:

"Though the fig tree may not blossom, Nor fruit be on the vines; Though the labor of the olive may fail, And the fields yield no food; Though the flock may be cut off from the fold, And there be no herd in the stalls Yet I will rejoice in the LORD, I will joy in the God of my salvation" (Habakkuk 3:17-18).

In other words, even when it looks like things haven't worked out, I would still choose to honor God and believe His Word than trust in any other resources. I am confident that every obstacle, challenge, and trial is subject to change. I refuse to sign on the dotted line or accept the delivery of a package assigned from the devil in the form of sickness, disease, or poverty. I will pray and seek God, and then I will praise Him until I receive the breakthrough. I will align my confession to what the Word of God says and I will not accept delivery for any package that contradicts what God's Word says about me. Return to sender!

It's easier to get someone else to pray! People have stopped praying for themselves as they find it more convenient to ask someone else to pray for them. I believe in the prayer of agreement, and it's good to have someone to stand with you in faith.

"Again I say to you that if two of you agree on earth concerning anything that they ask, it will be done for them by My Father in heaven." (Matthew 18:19).

Thank God for friends who will stand in faith agreement with you. However, you cannot relinquish your responsibility to pray for yourself.

A prayerless life is a lukewarm one! When a person neglects prayer it is evidence of a lukewarm heart. These Christians need a fresh encounter with God, and they need to place their lives on His altar as a living sacrifice. I am confident that if they draw near to God in prayer then He will draw near to them.

Therefore, submit to God. Resist the devil and he will flee from you. Draw near to God and He will draw near to you. Cleanse your hands, you sinners; and purify your hearts, you double-minded. Lament and mourn and weep! Let your laughter be turned to mourning and your joy to gloom. Humble yourselves in the sight of the Lord, and He will lift you up (James 4:7-10).

Believers who are passionate and are constantly in the pursuit of God's will for their lives are praying Christians.

Prayer Promises

Grace and peace be multiplied to you in the knowledge of God and of Jesus our Lord, as His divine power has given to us all things that pertain to life and godliness, through the knowledge of Him who called us by glory and virtue, by which have been given to us exceedingly great and precious promises, that through these you may be partakers of the divine nature, having escaped the corruption that is in the world through lust. (2 Peter 1:2-4)

"For all the promises of God in Him are Yes, and in Him Amen, to the glory of God through us" (2 Corinthians 1:20).

I want to share some great promises found in the Bible that will build your faith to receive answered prayer. Remember, it is not praying that will get results, but it is praying in faith. The only boundaries that exist that can limit your prayers are those of unbelief and small thinking. God is able to do exceedingly abundantly above all that we can ask (in prayer) or think.

"But Jesus looked at them and said to them, 'With men this is impossible, but with God all things are possible'" (Matthew 19:26).

"Jesus said to him, 'If you can believe, all things are possible to him who believes'" (Mark 9:23).

"So Jesus said to them, 'Because of your unbelief; for assuredly, I say to you, if you have faith as a mustard seed, you will say to this mountain, "Move from here to there," and it will move; and nothing will be impossible for you'" (Matthew 17:20).

"Call to Me, and I will answer you, and show you great and mighty things, which you do not know" (Jeremiah 33:3).

"Is anyone among you suffering? Let him pray. Is anyone cheerful? Let him sing psalms. Is anyone among you sick? Let him call for the elders of the church, and let them pray over him, anointing him with oil in the name of the Lord. And the prayer of faith will save the sick, and the Lord will raise him up. And if he has committed sins, he will be forgiven. Confess your trespasses to one another, and pray for one another, that you may be healed. The effective, fervent prayer of a righteous man avails much. Elijah was a man with a nature like ours, and he prayed earnestly that it would not rain; and it did not rain on the land for three years and six months. And he prayed again, and the heaven gave rain, and the earth produced its fruit" (James 5:13-18).

"A final word: Be strong in the Lord and in his mighty power. Put on all of God's armor so that you will be able to stand firm against all strategies of the devil. For we are not fighting against flesh-and-blood enemies, but against evil rulers and authorities of the unseen world, against mighty powers in this dark world, and against evil spirits in the heavenly places. Therefore, put on every piece of God's armor so you will be able to resist the enemy in the time of evil. Then after the battle, you will still be standing firm. Stand your ground, putting on the belt of truth and the body armor of God's righteousness. For shoes, put on the peace that comes from the Good News so that you will be fully prepared. In addition to all of these, hold up the shield of faith to stop the fiery arrows of the devil. Put on salvation as your helmet, and take the sword of the Spirit, which is the word of God. Pray in the Spirit at all times and on every occasion. Stay alert and be persistent in your prayers for all believers everywhere. And pray for me, too. Ask God to give me the right words so I can boldly explain God's mysterious plan that the Good News is for Jews and Gentiles alike. I am in chains now, still preaching this message as God's ambassador. So pray that I will keep on speaking boldly for him, as I should" (Ephesians 6:10-20).

"So I say to you, ask, and it will be given to you; seek, and you will find; knock, and it will be opened to you. For everyone who asks receives, and he who seeks finds, and to him who knocks it will be opened" (Luke 11:9-10).

"Most assuredly, I say to you, he who believes in Me, the works that I do he will do also; and greater works than these he will do, because I go to My Father. And whatever you ask in My name, that I will do, that the Father may be glorified in the Son" (John 14:12-13).

"Now this is the confidence that we have in Him, that if we ask anything according to His will, He hears us. And if we know that He hears us, whatever we ask, we know that we have the petitions that we have asked of Him" (1 John 5:14-15).

"So Jesus answered and said to them, 'Have faith in God. For assuredly, I say to you, whoever says to this mountain, "Be removed and be cast into the sea," and does not doubt in his heart, but believes that those things he says will come to pass, he will have whatever he says. Therefore, I say to you, whatever things you ask when you pray, believe that you receive them, and you will have them'" (Mark 11:22-24).

"And the prayer of faith will save the sick, and the Lord will raise him up. And if he has committed sins, he will be forgiven" (James 5:15).

"The eyes of the LORD are on the righteous, and His ears are open to their cry. The face of the LORD is against those who do evil, to cut off the remembrance of them from the earth. The righteous cry out, and the LORD hears, and delivers them out of all their troubles. The LORD is near to those who have a broken heart, and saves such as have a contrite spirit. Many are the afflictions of the righteous, but the LORD delivers him out of them all" (Psalm 34:15-19).

"And whatever you ask in My name, that I will do, that the Father may be glorified in the Son" (John 14:13).

"If you then, being evil, know how to give good gifts to your children, how much more will your heavenly Father give the Holy Spirit to those who ask Him!" (Luke 11:13).

"And in that day you will ask Me nothing. Most assuredly, I say to you, whatever you ask the Father in My name He will give you" (John 16:23).

"The LORD is far from the wicked, but He hears the prayer of the righteous" (Proverbs 15:29).

We are looking at praying bold prayers. I want to share a few examples of people who prayed bold prayers and God answered them. Remember, God who answered these prayers will do the same for you.

Moses prayed a BOLD prayer:

Then Moses said to the Lord, "See, You say to me, 'Bring up this people.' But You have not let me know whom You will send with me. Yet You have said, 'I know you by name, and you have also found grace in My sight.' Now therefore, I pray, if I have found grace in Your sight, show me now Your way, that I may know You and that I may find grace in Your sight. And consider that this nation is Your people." And He said, "My Presence will go with you, and I will give you rest." Then he said to Him, "If Your Presence does not go with us, do not bring us up from here. For how then will it be known that Your people and I have found grace in Your sight, except You go with us? So we shall be separate, Your people and I, from all the people who are upon the face of the earth." So the Lord said to Moses, "I will also do this thing that you have spoken; for you have found grace in My sight, and I know you by name." And he said, "Please, show me Your glory." Then He said, "I will make all My goodness pass before you, and I will proclaim the name of the Lord before you. I will be gracious to whom I will be gracious, and I will have compassion on whom I will have compassion." But He said, "You cannot see My face; for no man shall see Me, and live." And the Lord said, "Here is a place by Me, and you shall stand on the rock. So it shall be, while My glory passes by, that I will put you in the cleft of the rock, and will cover you with My hand while I pass by. Then I will take away My hand, and you shall see My back; but My face shall not be seen" (Exodus 33: 12-23).

Moses was a God-desperate man and leader. He realized that unless God was with him manifesting His glory that he was unable to get the task completed. He asked God for 3 things:

- Show me your way

- Manifest your presence

- Show me your glory

God said that He would fulfill these bold prayers with the exception that God would not show His face to Moses.

The early Church prayed with boldness requesting the infilling of power that God would be glorified through signs, wonders, and miracles.

In the face of open and violent persecution, they did not pray to escape but that God would grant them boldness and increased anointing to preach, cast out demons, heal the sick, and to work miracles. Their bold prayer was for boldness to increase for the advancement of the Gospel.

So when they heard that, they raised their voice to God with one accord and said: "Lord, You are God, who made heaven and earth and the sea, and all that is in them, who by the mouth of Your servant David have said: 'Why did the nations rage, and the people plot vain things? The kings of the earth took their stand, and the rulers were gathered together against the LORD and against His Christ.' "For truly against Your holy Servant Jesus, whom You anointed, both Herod and Pontius Pilate, with the Gentiles and the people of Israel, were gathered together to do whatever Your hand and Your purpose determined before to be done. Now, Lord, look on their threats, and grant to Your servants that with all boldness they may speak Your word, by stretching out Your hand to heal, and that signs and wonders may be done through the name of Your holy Servant Jesus." And when they had prayed, the place where they were assembled together was shaken; and they were all filled with the Holy Spirit, and they spoke the word of God with boldness (Acts 4:24-31).

Nehemiah prayed a BOLD prayer and asked God for favor with the king; God heard and answered his request. The impossible took place when Nehemiah prayed because God made a way for him to be released from the service as the king's cupbearer to lead the project to rebuild Jerusalem.

"'O Lord, I pray, please let Your ear be attentive to the prayer of Your servant, and to the prayer of Your servants who desire to fear Your name; and let Your servant prosper this day, I pray, and grant him mercy in the sight of this man.' For I was the king's cupbearer" (Nehemiah 1:11).

Jabez prayed a BOLD prayer and asked God for a changed reputation and favor. God heard and answered:

"And Jabez called on the God of Israel saying, 'Oh, that You would bless me indeed, and enlarge my territory, that Your hand would be with me, and that You would keep me from evil, that I may not cause pain!' So God granted him what he requested" (1 Chronicles 4:10).

Bold in Prayer

Elijah prayed a BOLD prayer for rain. God heard and answered. As a result of his bold prayers, the people were revived, and God saved them from idolatry.

> And the prayer of faith will save the sick, and the Lord will raise him up. And if he has committed sins, he will be forgiven. Confess your trespasses to one another, and pray for one another, that you may be healed. The effective, fervent prayer of a righteous man avails much. Elijah was a man with a nature like ours, and he prayed earnestly that it would not rain; and it did not rain on the land for three years and six months (James 5:15-17).

In the parable of the persistent widow, we learn that she made a very BOLD request, and she never backed down until the judge made provision for her request:

> Then He spoke a parable to them, that men always ought to pray and not lose heart, saying: "There was in a certain city a judge who did not fear God nor regard man. Now there was a widow in that city; and she came to him, saying, 'Get justice for me from my adversary.' And he would not for a while; but afterward he said within himself, 'Though I do not fear God nor regard man, yet because this widow troubles me I will avenge her, lest by her continual coming she weary me.'" Then the Lord said, "Hear what the unjust judge said. And shall God not avenge His own elect who cry out day and night to Him, though He bears long with them? I tell you that He

31

will avenge them speedily. Nevertheless, when the Son of Man comes, will He really find faith on the earth?" (Luke 18:1-8).

The Roman Centurion made a BOLD request to Jesus, and his BOLD faith obtained a miracle:

Now when Jesus had entered Capernaum, a centurion came to Him, pleading with Him, saying, "Lord, my servant is lying at home paralyzed, dreadfully tormented." And Jesus said to him, "I will come and heal him." The centurion answered and said, "Lord, I am not worthy that You should come under my roof. But only speak a word, and my servant will be healed. For I also am a man under authority, having soldiers under me. And I say to this one, 'Go,' and he goes; and to another, 'Come,' and he comes; and to my servant, 'Do this,' and he does it." When Jesus heard it, He marveled, and said to those who followed, "Assuredly, I say to you, I have not found such great faith, not even in Israel! And I say to you that many will come from east and west, and sit down with Abraham, Isaac, and Jacob in the kingdom of heaven. But the sons of the kingdom will be cast out into outer darkness. There will be weeping and gnashing of teeth." Then Jesus said to the centurion, "Go your way; and as you have believed, so let it be done for you." And his servant was healed that same hour (Matthew 8:5-13).

The Church prayed with boldness all night and requested that Peter be released from prison; their request was answered:

> Peter was therefore kept in prison, but constant prayer was offered to God for him by the Church. And when Herod was about to bring him out, that night Peter was sleeping, bound with two chains between two soldiers; and the guards before the door were keeping the prison. Now behold, an angel of the Lord stood by him, and a light shone in the prison; and he struck Peter on the side and raised him up, saying, "Arise quickly!" And his chains fell off his hands. Then the angel said to him, "Gird yourself and tie on your sandals"; and so he did. And he said to him, "Put on your garment and follow me." So he went out and followed him, and did not know that what was done by the angel was real, but thought he was seeing a vision. When they were past the first and the second guard posts, they came to the iron gate that leads to the city, which opened to them of its own accord; and they went out and went down one street, and immediately the angel departed from him.
>
> And when Peter had come to himself, he said, "Now I know for certain that the Lord has sent His angel, and has delivered me from the hand of Herod and from all the expectation of the Jewish people." So, when he had considered this, he came to the house of Mary, the mother of John whose surname was Mark, where many were gathered together praying. And as Peter

knocked at the door of the gate, a girl named Rhoda
came to answer. When she recognized Peter's voice,
because of her gladness she did not open the gate, but
ran in and announced that Peter stood before the
gate. But they said to her, "You are beside yourself!"
Yet she kept insisting that it was so. So they said, "It is
his angel."

Now Peter continued knocking; and when they
opened the door and saw him, they were
astonished. But motioning to them with his hand to
keep silent, he declared to them how the Lord had
brought him out of the prison. And he said, "Go, tell
these things to James and to the brethren." And he
departed and went to another place (Acts 12:5-17).

What Bold prayers can we ask?

Ask for the Nations

"Ask of Me, and I will give You The nations for Your
inheritance, And the ends of the earth for Your
possession" (Psalm 2:8).

Ask for Miracles

"Now, Lord, look on their threats, and grant to Your
servants that with all boldness they may speak Your
word, by stretching out Your hand to heal, and that signs
and wonders may be done through the name of Your
holy Servant Jesus" (Acts 4:29-30).

Ask for Workers

"Then he said to his disciples, 'The harvest is plentiful, but the laborers are few; therefore, pray earnestly to the Lord of the harvest to send out laborers into his harvest'" (Luke 9:37).

Ask for Good Rulers and Authorities

"'Therefore I exhort first of all that supplications, prayers, intercessions, and giving of thanks be made for all men, for kings and all who are in authority, that we may lead a quiet and peaceable life in all godliness and reverence. For this is good and acceptable in the sight of God our Savior" (1 Timothy 2:1-3).

Ask for Wisdom

"If any of you lacks wisdom, let him ask of God, who gives to all liberally and without reproach, and it will be given to him" (James 1:5).

Ask for Doors of Opportunity to Minister

"…meanwhile praying also for us, that God would open to us a door for the word, to speak the mystery of Christ, for which I am also in chains" (Colossians 4:3).

Ask anything, no limits, no selfishness but bold faith

"And whatever you ask in My name, that I will do, that the Father may be glorified in the Son" (John 14:13).

Chapter 3

Bold Faith

A Nasty Email from a Bible Student

I recently received an email from one of my eBible Institute Students accusing me of promoting a heretical teacher and false doctrine. She was referring to just one quote from Kenneth Copeland about faith, in just one of the modules.

To put this in context, I quote John McArthur occasionally in my writings, but that does not mean I carte blanche endorse everything that he says or teaches. In fact, I have some major disagreements with his opposition to the baptism in the Spirit and speaking in other tongues. However, he has a brilliant grasp of some major biblical truths, and I agree with a lot that he teaches.

Back to Kenneth Copeland – I don't think that he is a heretic, in fact, I love his teachings. In my early years of growth and ministry, I listened prolifically to his "tapes" (some of you won't know what tapes are – these preceded CD's and DVD's) and read all his books, his teachings have taught me much concerning faith, ministry, leadership, and life.

Again, if I may make this statement with all sincerity, do I agree with 100% of what he has said or taught? Probably not, BUT I don't even agree with all that I have said and taught. Over the many years of ministry, I have grown in the knowledge of the Word and other skills. I wish I could get rid of some of my old teachings. All preachers say things that don't always come out the way we intended. We all dig holes that we can't seem to get out of or we go off on some rabbit trail and get lost in the process.

My dear eBible Institute student is facing major challenges—her life is an utter mess. She has a dysfunctional home and marriage; her health is bad, and she is bankrupt. She needs desperate help from God; she needs a miracle. In my opinion, she should be trying to access everything that Kenneth Copeland has taught, rather than criticizing him. I would, if I was in her place, try to get everything that would help me grow in faith. I would study how to get a breakthrough in the realm of faith. Rather than criticize the message of faith we should explore and become bold in.

1. We need bold faith to accomplish the task of reaching our generation.

2. We need bold faith to awaken the gifts of the Spirit to flow in FULL power and see signs, wonders, and miracles.

3. We need bold faith to obtain the resources of heaven for the harvest.

It is sad that many leaders have taken precious time to teach contradictory messages concerning faith. In fact, their criticism of faith has formed an alliance with hell.

Bold Faith

The devil and his agents oppose faith because people with bold faith are the ones who are doing the work of God and living sacrificially for the Gospel. I have learned that bold faith is impressive to Jesus—I want to impress Him!

The Roman Centurion

Now when Jesus had entered Capernaum, a centurion came to Him, pleading with Him, saying, "Lord, my servant is lying at home paralyzed, dreadfully tormented." And Jesus said to him, "I will come and heal him." The centurion answered and said, "Lord, I am not worthy that You should come under my roof. But only speak a word, and my servant will be healed. For I also am a man under authority, having soldiers under me. And I say to this one, 'Go,' and he goes; and to another, 'Come,' and he comes; and to my servant, 'Do this,' and he does it." When Jesus heard it, He marveled, and said to those who followed, "Assuredly, I say to you, I have not found such great faith, not even in Israel! And I say to you that many will come from east and west, and sit down with Abraham, Isaac, and Jacob in the kingdom of heaven. But the sons of the kingdom will be cast out into outer darkness. There will be weeping and gnashing of teeth." Then Jesus said to the centurion, "Go your way; and as you have believed, so let it be done for you." And his servant was healed that same hour (Matthew 8:5-13).

This Roman Centurion impressed Jesus with two things:

1.   His bold faith.

2. His deep sense of honor for Jesus and the authority that he exercised.

I would rather Jesus say to me, "You have great faith" than say to me, "Oh you of little faith." Bold faith honors and receives from God.

"Now faith is the assurance of things hoped for, the conviction of things not seen" (Hebrew 11:1).

Some people have faith in other persons, religions or idols. As Christians, we have faith in God. The scripture tells us that we must have faith in God and in the Gospels, Jesus Himself calls on us to exercise such faith. When we understand that even a little faith can move a mountain, then we can grasp the power of bold faith accomplishing all that God places in our hearts.

So Jesus answered and said to them, 'Have faith in God. For assuredly, I say to you, whoever says to this mountain, 'Be removed and be cast into the sea,' and does not doubt in his heart, but believes that those things he says will be done, he will have whatever he says. Therefore, I say to you, whatever things you ask when you pray, believe that you receive them, and you will have them (Mark 11:22-24).

What is the difference between bold faith and little faith?

I want to reference a few Scriptures to show you what bold faith looks like and the principles people operating with bold faith use. I will also share some Scriptures

40

where there is little faith exhibited and what we can learn from these biblical events. Ultimately, I trust that you will stir yourself in your most holy faith and contend for the faith that was delivered to the saints of old. I will attempt to adequately articulate the difference between bold faith and little faith, and help you pursue bold faith.

People who worry about their daily needs are those who have little faith. They are moved by the circumstances of life, rather than the promises found in the Word of God.

For this reason, I say to you, do not be worried about your life, as to what you will eat or what you will drink; nor for your body, as to what you will put on. Is not life more than food, and the body more than clothing? "Look at the birds of the air, that they do not sow, nor reap nor gather into barns, and yet your heavenly Father feeds them. Are you not worth much more than they? "And who of you by being worried can add a single hour to his life? "And why are you worried about clothing? Observe how the lilies of the field grow; they do not toil nor do they spin, yet I say to you that not even Solomon in all his glory clothed himself like one of these. "But if God so clothes the grass of the field, which is alive today and tomorrow is thrown into the furnace, will He not much more clothe you? You of little faith! "Do not worry then, saying, 'What will we eat?' or 'What will we drink?' or 'What will we wear for clothing?' "For the Gentiles eagerly seek all these things; for your heavenly Father knows that you need all these things.

41

"But seek first His kingdom and His righteousness, and all these things will be added to you. "So do not worry about tomorrow; for tomorrow will care for itself. Each day has enough trouble of its own" (Matthew 6:25-34).

People who panic in storms are operating in little faith. They are moved by what is happening around them rather than living the reality of God in them, with them and for them.

When He got into the boat, His disciples followed Him. And behold, there arose a great storm on the sea, so that the boat was being covered with the waves, but Jesus Himself was asleep. And they came to Him and woke Him, saying, "Save us, Lord; we are perishing!" He said to them, "Why are you afraid, you men of little faith?" Then He got up and rebuked the winds and the sea, and it became perfectly calm. The men were amazed, and said, "What kind of a man is this, that even the winds and the sea obey Him?" (Matthew 8:23-27).

Little faith is stifled by fear while great faith is amplified by boldness.

Peter shows us how fear hinders the operation of faith. Remember, Peter was walking on the water, but when he allowed his focus to be turned away from Jesus to the environment, he began to sink. Though he started out boldly, fear stifled his faith, and he began to sink.

Immediately He made the disciples get into the boat and go ahead of Him to the other side while He sent the crowds away. After He had sent the crowds away, He went up on the mountain by Himself to pray; and when it was evening, He was there alone. But the boat was already a long distance from the land, battered by the waves; for the wind was contrary. And in the fourth watch of the night, He came to them, walking on the sea. When the disciples saw Him walking on the sea, they were terrified, and said, "It is a ghost!" And they cried out in fear. But immediately Jesus spoke to them, saying, "Take courage, it is I; do not be afraid." Peter said to Him, "Lord, if it is You, command me to come to You on the water." And He said, "Come!" And Peter got out of the boat, and walked on the water and came toward Jesus. But seeing the wind, he became frightened, and beginning to sink, he cried out, "Lord, save me!" Immediately Jesus stretched out His hand and took hold of him, and said to him, "You of little faith, why did you doubt?" When they got into the boat, the wind stopped. And those who were in the boat worshiped Him, saying, "You are certainly God's Son!" (Matthew 14:22-33).

People of little faith are those who are spiritually insensitive and fail to understand what God is saying.

And the disciples came to the other side of the sea, but they had forgotten to bring any bread. And Jesus said to them, "Watch out and beware of the leaven of the

Pharisees and Sadducees." They began to discuss this among themselves, saying, "He said that because we did not bring any bread." But Jesus, aware of this, said, "You men of little faith, why do you discuss among yourselves that you have no bread? "Do you not yet understand or remember the five loaves of the five thousand, and how many baskets full you picked up? "Or the seven loaves of the four thousand, and how many large baskets full you picked up? "How is it that you do not understand that I did not speak to you concerning bread? But beware of the leaven of the Pharisees and Sadducees." Then they understood that He did not say to beware of the leaven of bread, but of the teaching of the Pharisees and Sadducees (Matthew 16:5-12).

People who are weak in spiritual authority are operating in little faith.

When they came to the crowd, a man came up to Jesus, falling on his knees before Him and saying, "Lord, have mercy on my son, for he is a lunatic and is very ill; for he often falls into the fire and often into the water. "I brought him to Your disciples, and they could not cure him." And Jesus answered and said, "You unbelieving and perverted generation, how long shall I be with you? How long shall I put up with you? Bring him here to Me." And Jesus rebuked him, and the demon came out of him, and the boy was cured at once. Then the disciples came to Jesus privately and said, "Why could we not drive it out?" And He said to

* Bold Faith *

them, "Because of the littleness of your faith; for truly I say to you, if you have faith the size of a mustard seed, you will say to this mountain, 'Move from here to there,' and it will move; and nothing will be impossible to you (Matthew 17:14-20).

Bold faith partners with honor

And when Jesus entered Capernaum, a centurion came to Him, imploring Him, and saying, "Lord, my servant is lying paralyzed at home, fearfully tormented." Jesus said to him, "I will come and heal him." But the centurion said, "Lord, I am not worthy for You to come under my roof, but just say the word, and my servant will be healed. "For I also am a man under authority, with soldiers under me; and I say to this one, 'Go!' and he goes, and to another, 'Come!' and he comes, and to my slave, 'Do this!' and he does it." Now when Jesus heard this, He marveled and said to those who were following, "Truly I say to you, I have not found such great faith with anyone in Israel. "I say to you that many will come from east and west, and recline at the table with Abraham, Isaac and Jacob in the kingdom of heaven; but the sons of the kingdom will be cast out into the outer darkness; in that place there will be weeping and gnashing of teeth." And Jesus said to the centurion, "Go; it shall be done for you as you have believed." And the servant was healed that very moment (Matthew 8:5-13)

BOLD

Bold faith takes radical risks and accomplishes the impossible!

Getting into a boat, Jesus crossed over the sea and came to His own city. And they brought to Him a paralytic lying on a bed. Seeing their faith, Jesus said to the paralytic, "Take courage, son; your sins are forgiven." And some of the scribes said to themselves, "This fellow blasphemes." And Jesus knowing their thoughts said, "Why are you thinking evil in your hearts? "Which is easier, to say, 'Your sins are forgiven,' or to say, 'Get up, and walk'? "But so that you may know that the Son of Man has authority on earth to forgive sins"—then He said to the paralytic, "Get up, pick up your bed and go home." And he got up and went home. But when the crowds saw this, they were awestruck, and glorified God, who had given such authority to men (Matthew 9:1-8).

Bold faith presses through the crowd and gets to Jesus.

While He was saying these things to them, a synagogue official came and bowed down before Him, and said, "My daughter has just died; but come and lay Your hand on her, and she will live." Jesus got up and began to follow him, and so did His disciples. And a woman who had been suffering from a hemorrhage for twelve years, came up behind Him and touched the fringe of His cloak; for she was saying to herself, "If I only touch His garment, I will get well." But Jesus turning and seeing her said,

"Daughter, take courage; your faith has made you well." At once the woman was made well. (Matthew 9:18-22)

The woman with the issue of blood boldly went forward and touched Jesus. She didn't wait to be invited forward; she knew that she would never get to Him if she waited. She boldly acted, took a risk and crawled through all the people until she got to the edge of His garment. As she touched Jesus' garment, her faith was released and divine virtue flowed into her body.

Bold faith doesn't back away but dares to get Jesus' attention.

As Jesus went on from there, two blind men followed Him, crying out, "Have mercy on us, Son of David!" When He entered the house, the blind men came up to Him, and Jesus said to them, "Do you believe that I am able to do this?" They said to Him, "Yes, Lord." Then He touched their eyes, saying, "It shall be done to you according to your faith." And their eyes were opened. And Jesus sternly warned them: "See that no one knows about this!" But they went out and spread the news about Him throughout all that land (Matthew 9:27-31).

Great faith operates in spiritual wisdom

Jesus went away from there, and withdrew into the district of Tyre and Sidon. And a Canaanite woman from that region came out and began to cry out, saying, "Have mercy on me, Lord, Son of David; my daughter is cruelly demon-possessed." But He did not answer her a word. And His disciples came and implored Him, saying, "Send her away, because she keeps shouting at us." But He answered and said, "I was sent only to the lost sheep of the house of Israel." But she came and began to bow down before Him, saying, "Lord, help me!" And He answered and said, "It is not good to take the children's bread and throw it to the dogs." But she said, "Yes, Lord; but even the dogs feed on the crumbs which fall from their masters' table." Then Jesus said to her, "O woman, your faith is great; it shall be done for you as you wish." And her daughter was healed at once (Matthew 15:21-28).

The blind men boldly cried out and followed Jesus; they made their way uninvited into the house seeking healing. They were not going to be silenced or pushed aside. They were desperate and they were bold. This principle of being desperate and bold is critical to grasp. If a person is desperate but not bold they may succumb to being silenced, and in the process miss their divine encounter.

The same can be said for the Canaanite woman who was bold enough to break all protocol and approached the Jewish Jesus appealing for her daughter's healing. As you can see in both instances, that bold faith pressed through the barriers—cultural and physical and made their way to Jesus.

Bold Faith

Little faith makes decisions based on what is possible for humans while great faith makes decisions based on what is possible for God.

In Mark 2:4, we read about the friends who boldly tore open a roof to lower their friend to the feet of Jesus. They were not going to allow their friend to miss his miracle just because the house was too crowded. Bold people find a way to get to Jesus. They are not easily turned away by obstacles.

So, in light of what we've read, let us pursue bold faith:

1. Boldly go after all that you are seeking to accomplish in the Spirit.

2. Have your eyes fixed on Jesus and realize that the spiritual world that is ruled by God is accessible to you through faith. Let your heart be established in the principles of the Word of God and don't allow external limitations and obstacles to prevent you obtaining from God what is needed.

3. Make your decisions based on what is possible for God and not what you see, feel or hear. Be governed by the Word and not by your environment.

In doing these things, may it be said of us, "O you of great faith!" Bold faith brings pleasure to the heart of God. Some critical Christians may misunderstand you

BOLD

and even criticize you, but remember, God applauds your bold faith.

Chapter 4

Bold Witness

A deep sense of urgency should grip the heart of every Christian concerning the mandate to reach the lost. When Peter stood and began to quote from the prophet Joel on the Day of Pentecost, he made this statement, "And it shall come to pass in the last days, says God, That I will pour out of My Spirit on all flesh" (Acts 2:17a). The last days began when the Spirit was poured out on the Day of Pentecost. Therefore, it is safe to say that we are now living in the closing seconds of the last days. Jesus said that before He returned the Gospel would be preached in all nations.

"And He said to them, "It is not for you to know times or seasons which the Father has put in His own authority. But you shall receive power when the Holy Spirit has come upon you; and you shall be witnesses to Me in Jerusalem, and in all Judea and Samaria, and to the end of the earth" (Acts 1:7-8).

The empowering of the believers on the Day of Pentecost was for the spread of the Gospel. The message of salvation would be preached from Jerusalem to the ends of the earth. Every believer needs this empowering of the Spirit. We are called to spread the Gospel, therefore, we all need boldness from on high. The priority of every Christian must be taking the responsibility of carrying the Gospel to this generation. The work of world evangelism must be accomplished before the return of

51

the Lord Jesus. Notice that I said, every Christian. I did not say every evangelist, pastor or missionary. The task of the harvest is not the responsibility of a select few who are called, but we are all called to this great mandate. For those who are afraid of being rejected, or for those who feel that they are not bold enough to share the Gospel, this is a good verse for you:

Cry out to God for Boldness

"In the day when I cried out, You answered me, And made me bold with strength in my soul" (Psalm 138:3).

Today is a good day to seek God for boldness. The Psalmist said, "In the day when I cried out." I suggested that you do it today because I don't want you to get distracted from having an encounter with God. If God touches your life, you will be changed forever. If you need boldness, then today is a good time to seek God for a holy download.

Often people will cry out to God in times of distress or trouble. However, for this exercise, I want to suggest that you seek Him for the awakened potential to win the lost with the same dependence you have when you need help. I guess it is safe to say that we are living in perilous days, and we need God's empowerment to proclaim the Gospel. Everything seems to be trying to mute the Church from reaching the lost.

The second observation from this verse is the deep sense of passion in David's appeal. It says that he cried out to

God. The words "cried out" means to shout. When I read this verse, I hear the cry of passion and not desperation. Some cry out in despair, but we also need to cry out with hearts that blaze with passion.

Sad to say, some Christians have lost their first love. With this loss of passion, many believers drift with the rise and fall of the tide. These carnal believers are moved by the waves generated by the weather, rather than being moved by the Holy Spirit.

When the psalmist cried out to God, two things happened:

1. God answered his cry.

2. God gave him boldness in the depth of his being. This boldness gave David the inner strength required to face the challenges of life and leadership.

If you seek God with passion right now, the God who heard David will hear you. God, who gave David boldness, will also give you boldness in the core of your being. If you are ignited with holy fire in your heart, you will not be ashamed of the Gospel. You will boldly proclaim the message of life to all who will hear you. Bold Christians are not embarrassed to share the good news of salvation.

"Therefore do not be ashamed of the testimony of our Lord, nor of me His prisoner, but share with me in the sufferings for the gospel according to the power of God" (2 Timothy 1:8).

Peter and John were Bold in the Gospel

Peter and John were bold in the Gospel and flowing in the power of God. In fact, preaching the Gospel and operating in the power of God are synonymous. These two always go together. The presentation of the Gospel is always in association with the power of God being demonstrated.

"Now when they saw the boldness of Peter and John, and perceived that they were uneducated and untrained men, they marveled. And they realized that they had been with Jesus" (Acts 4:13).

Peter and John were bold for a number of reasons:

Jesus had taught, trained and modeled for them how to operate in the power of God. When you spend extensive time with anyone—in this case with Jesus, then you will find an impartation taking place. Jesus not only taught them, but He gave them His heart and confidence.

"These two men were in the upper room and received the Baptism in the Holy Spirit. They were made bold by the empowerment of God" (Acts 1:8).

The Pharisees had to acknowledge that these two men were bold because they had been with Jesus. Though they were not taught and trained in the classical method, they were not uneducated. They had been with the teacher above all teachers. They spent almost three years in the school of Jesus. They were not only taught the Word; they were taught by the Word.

Never doubt your inclusion in the promises of God

I want you to observe that Jesus had the ability to heal, feed and empower all those who came to Him. He not only met the needs of those who came to Him. Jesus also empowered and commissioned them all. You are included in this empowerment and commission.

Jesus healed all the people

"When evening had come, they brought to Him many who were demon-possessed. And He cast out the spirits with a word, and healed all who were sick" (Matthew 8:16).

Jesus fed all the people

Then He commanded the multitudes to sit down on the grass. And He took the five loaves and the two fish, and looking up to heaven, He blessed and broke and gave the loaves to the disciples; and the disciples gave to the multitudes. So they all ate and were filled, and they took up twelve baskets full of the fragments that remained. Now those who had eaten were about five thousand men, besides women and children (Matthew 14:19-21).

BOLD

The Holy Spirit filled all the believers

And suddenly there came a sound from heaven, as of a rushing mighty wind, and it filled the whole house where they were sitting. Then there appeared to them divided tongues, as of fire, and one sat upon each of them. And they were all filled with the Holy Spirit and began to speak with other tongues, as the Spirit gave them utterance (Acts 2:2-4).

Every believer was mobilized in the power of God

Now, Lord, look on their threats, and grant to Your servants that with all boldness they may speak Your word, by stretching out Your hand to heal, and that signs and wonders may be done through the name of Your holy Servant Jesus." And when they had prayed, the place where they were assembled together was shaken; and they were all filled with the Holy Spirit, and they spoke the word of God with boldness (Acts 4:29-31).

In the face of severe opposition, threats, persecution, and conflict, the apostles and the people prayed for boldness to speak the Word of God. They also desired that the supernatural manifestation of healings and miracles would escalate.

4 Key elements to our witness:

1. The Declaration of the Gospel

How then shall they call on Him in whom they have not believed? And how shall they believe in Him of whom they have not heard? And how shall they hear without a preacher?

And how shall they preach unless they are sent? As it is written: "How beautiful are the feet of those who preach the gospel of peace, Who bring glad tidings of good things!" (Romans 10:14-15).

"They went everywhere preaching" (Mark 16:16).

Note it doesn't say that they went everywhere doing charity work or living morally—it says, they went everywhere preaching. Saving faith comes by hearing the message of life. When someone hears the Gospel, then faith is born in that person's heart. The Gospel becomes the incorruptible seed that produces the new birth.

"And this gospel of the kingdom will be preached in all the world as a witness to all the nations, and then the end will come" (Matthew 24:14).

2. The demonstration of the Gospel

"For our gospel did not come to you in word only, but also in power, and in the Holy Spirit and in much assurance, as you know what kind of men we were among you for your sake" (1 Thessalonians 1:5).

Signs followed the proclamation of the Gospel. As they went preaching, God was backing their message with signs.

"And these signs will follow those who believe: In My name they will cast out demons; they will speak with new tongues; they will take up serpents; and if they drink anything deadly, it will by no means hurt them; they will lay hands on the sick, and they will recover" (Mark 16:17-18).

The works that I do, you shall do also

"Most assuredly, I say to you, he who believes in Me, the works that I do he will do also; and greater works than these he will do, because I go to My Father" (John 14:12).

As the Father has sent me so send I you

"So Jesus said to them again, 'Peace to you! As the Father has sent Me, I also send you'" (John 20:21).

The Spirit of the Lord is upon us

The Spirit of the LORD is upon Me, Because He has anointed Me To preach the gospel to the poor; He has sent Me to heal the brokenhearted, To proclaim liberty to the captives And recovery of sight to the blind, To set at liberty those who are oppressed; To proclaim the acceptable year of the LORD" (Luke 4:18-19).

3. Our Conduct

I therefore, the prisoner for the Lord, appeal to and beg you to walk (lead a life) worthy of the [divine] calling to which you have been called [with behavior that is a credit to the summons to God's service, Living as becomes you] with complete lowliness of mind (humility) and meekness (unselfishness, gentleness, mildness), with patience, bearing with one another and making allowances because you love one another (Ephesians 4:1-2 AMP).

Don't live a different life to your message. The way you live with your family and friends is louder than your message. When you live your life with godly character those closest to you are more likely to ask you concerning your salvation.

"But in your hearts set Christ apart as holy [and acknowledge Him] as Lord. Always be ready to give a logical defense to anyone who asks you to account for the hope that is in you, but do it courteously and respectfully" (1 Peter 3:15 (AMP).

When we live a contradictory lifestyle to our message, we are setting up ourselves for criticism and even the unsaved will question the reality of our walk with God. They will question if we are truly saved. By saying this, I am not promoting a hyper-holiness lifestyle that implies we are saved through our own efforts and morality. We are saved by grace, and we are kept and sanctified by the grace of God. Sinless perfectionism is a vicious beast, and people who try to live in such a way are usually unable to consistently sustain themselves. On the other hand, I am not endorsing sloppy grace that places no obligation on the Christian to make the right choices in life. We are saved by grace through faith, and we are sanctified by grace and faith.

We as Christians ought to avoid sinful practices; we should pay our bills on time, we should work diligently and carry a good positive attitude. In our businesses, we should be hard-working, diligent, and creative. The way that we live and work should give evidence to the saving grace of God.

4. Our Compassion in Action

"Let your light so shine before men, that they may see your good works and glorify your Father in heaven" (Matthew 5:16).

Christian compassion reaches out and helps those in need. We are generous with our giving to widows, orphans and the elderly.

We care for those in the Church as demonstrated by the Corinthian Christians. They extended sacrificial giving to the saints in Jerusalem who were facing severe famine.

Now concerning the collection for the saints, as I have given orders to the churches of Galatia, so you must do also: On the first day of the week let each one of you lay something aside, storing up as he may prosper, that there be no collections when I come. And when I come, whomever you approve by your letters I will send to bear your gift to Jerusalem (1 Corinthians 16:1-3).

When the Apostles acknowledged Paul's ministry, they asked him to remember the poor. In response, he assured them that this too was his desire. Helping the suffering was a necessary ingredient of the Gospel.

"They desired only that we should remember the poor, the very thing which I also was eager to do" (Galatians 2:10).

The story of the good Samaritan is a parable (Luke 10:25-37) taught by Jesus as an example of the importance of helping those in desperate need. The good Samaritan went out of his way to care for the man lying in the ditch unable to help himself. The parable taught the disciples about compassion, generosity and going out of our way to help the helpless. Jesus concluded this parable with these words, "Go and do likewise" (Luke 10:37). The volume of our message will be amplified by our generosity and compassion to the suffering.

Go with Power!

"But you shall receive power when the Holy Spirit has come upon you; and you shall be witnesses to Me in Jerusalem, and in all Judea and Samaria, and to the end of the earth" (Acts 1:8).

We receive power when we are baptized in the Holy Spirit. This experience is specifically to empower the Church to be a witness. The purpose of the Holy Spirit's power is to enable us to carry out the same ministry Jesus did—preaching the good news, healing the sick, and delivering the oppressed. He is in heaven now, seated at the right hand of the Father, but He has equipped us to continue His work here on earth through the power of the Holy Spirit. Jesus was limited to being in one place at a time, but through the Holy Spirit in us, He can be everywhere because wherever we go, He goes. Our lives become the extension and the continuum of His ministry.

Pentecost, also known as the Feasts of Weeks (Leviticus 23:15-22), is the feast of harvest. God uniquely selected this day for the outpouring of the Holy Spirit. The Holy Spirit was given on that day because He is a soul-winning Spirit. When the 120 followers of Christ received the promise of the Spirit, they were totally transformed.

Once timid and fearful, Peter turned into an on-fire radical for Jesus. He immediately started going after souls, and as a result, his bold preaching brought in the harvest of 3,000 people who were saved (Acts 2:41). From that day onward, Jesus' followers were unstoppable, going everywhere preaching the Gospel even in the face of great persecution and physical danger. Their God-given boldness enabled them to preach in the face of open hostility. Will you be unstoppable? We must be diligent about the harvest (John 4:35).

Do the work of the Evangelist

"But you be watchful in all things, endure afflictions, do the work of an evangelist, fulfill your ministry" (2 Timothy 4:5).

Some Christians are called to the office of an evangelist. (Ephesians 4:11). Evangelists have been given the ability to communicate the Gospel to individuals as well as large crowds. Billy Graham is a world-renowned evangelist. Other well-known evangelists from the past and present are Reinhard Bonnke, T.L. Osborne, and Oral Roberts. These men have all proclaimed the Gospel to millions of people around the globe.

The book of Acts records that Philip was an evangelist. Most evangelists will preach the Gospel with authority as well as operate in the divine ability to heal and perform miracles.

"On the next day we who were Paul's companions departed and came to Caesarea, and entered the house of Philip the evangelist, who was one of the seven, and stayed with him" (Acts 21:8).

According to Ephesians 4:11, one of the functions of the evangelist should also be to equip and train Christians to communicate the Gospel. Perhaps, one of the reasons we don't see the average Christian mobilized to win souls is because most evangelists are reaching large crowds but are not imparting this grace to the saints. For the saints to effectively do the work of ministry, and specifically in this context to evangelize, they need impartation and training from the evangelist.

If you are not called to the office of an evangelist, you can still do the work of an evangelist. Some people are gifted to pray; they can intercede and seek God for hours because there is a special grace on them. However, all Christians should pray and intercede.

There are those believers who are uniquely gifted to be hospitable, but in essence, all Christians should be hospitable. In the same way, if you are called to a particular area of ministry, say prophecy, this doesn't mean that you should not reach the lost. You may focus on prophecy, but you can still do the work of an evangelist.

I know many pastors who are awesome at feeding and caring for the Church, but they are not involved in evangelism. If they don't get out and share the Gospel, they will have a good, well cared for church, but it won't be growing with new converts. It may grow through the movement of Christians from one church to another but, the Lord added to the Church daily through new births. What we need today is daily growth through new converts. To accomplish this, we need bold pastors and bold, trained church members.

Paul was bold in the Gospel

"For which I am an ambassador in chains; that in it I may speak boldly, as I ought to speak" (Ephesians 6:20).

We need the power of the Spirit to make us bold in the Gospel. Thousands of people who were at one stage bold and busy spreading the Gospel have become sterile and pastoral. We need a turnaround in the church. Ask God to fill you with the spirit of boldness so that you can preach the Gospel.

> How then shall they call on Him in whom they have not believed? And how shall they believe in Him of whom they have not heard? And how shall they hear without a preacher? And how shall they preach unless they are sent? As it is written: "How beautiful are the feet of those who preach the gospel of peace, Who bring glad tidings of good things!" (Romans 10:14-15).

How shall they hear without a preacher? Or, how shall they hear without a bold preacher? We need every Christian to be filled with the spirit of boldness so that the Word of God can be spread.

Chapter 5

Bold in the Spirit

"Not by might or power but by my Sprit says the Lord of Hosts" (Zechariah 4:6).

Everything I am about to share concerning operating in the Spirit with boldness is from the overflow of our personal and growing relationship with Jesus. It is essential to grasp that everything that we do is from that. We are not entrusted with the power of God or a ministry because of our potential, but because we love God and He loves us. Our authority and abilities are gifts that come from God. The operations of the gifts of the Spirit are not earned but are obtained by faith, and inspired by love—our love for God and His people.

I learned that one of the great secrets to operating in spiritual boldness is our ability to hear the voice of God. The second secret is our ability to see what God shows us. We must then obey or do what God has revealed.

You will observe these two secrets in the ministry of Jesus:

1. Hearing God

"Do you not believe that I am in the Father, and the Father in Me? The words that I speak to you I do not speak on My own authority; but the Father who dwells in Me does the works" (John 14:10).

2. Seeing what God shows you

> Then Jesus answered and said to them, "Most assuredly, I say to you, the Son can do nothing of Himself, but what He sees the Father do; for whatever He does, the Son also does in like manner. For the Father loves the Son, and shows Him all things that He Himself does; and He will show Him greater works than these, that you may marvel. For as the Father raises the dead and gives life to them, even so the Son gives life to whom He will. (John 5:19-21).

Once you have heard and seen, then, you have to obey. You receive the clear voice of God or you see what God reveals and then with boldness, you follow and do all that He has shared with you. Hearing and seeing flows from the secret place where we commune with God. It is here, in the secret place, that God shares His heart with yours; His will becomes yours, and you align your plans to His calling.

Our gifting is not dependent on maturity, knowledge or experience. In other words, a young Christian can flow in the power of God. These immature Christians may not have worked out some of the issues in their lives, and they may not even have acquired much biblical knowledge. An example of this is the Corinthian church, the members had problems and were immature, but they flowed in the gifts of the Spirit. Though it is ideal that those who operate in the power of God must be mature and have sound biblical training. It is also essential that they possess godly character, but don't be surprised when a young believer flows in the gifts and still has a lot of growing to do.

The subject of flowing in the gifts is not limited to missionaries, pastors, or evangelists, but it is available to everyone who is born of God. Every Christian is to be Spirit-filled. This experience is not restricted to certain denominations or movements. The promise of the Holy Spirit was given to all Christians from Pentecost to the return of Jesus.

"Then Peter said to them, 'Repent, and let every one of you be baptized in the name of Jesus Christ for the remission of sins; and you shall receive the gift of the Holy Spirit. For the promise is to you and to your children, and to all who are afar off, as many as the Lord our God will call'" (Acts 2:38-39).

As you can see from Acts 2:38-39, everyone who is saved is promised the baptism in the Holy Spirit. The entire context of Peter's sermon was around the upper room outpouring of the Holy Spirit. He was not merely alluding to this event as being limited to the 120 who were present. He was bold to say that what they had heard, and seen were for that generation and every subsequent generation until Jesus returns.

"And do not be drunk with wine, in which is dissipation; but be filled with the Spirit" (Ephesians 5:18).

Paul echoed this when he taught that everyone should be Spirit filled. When the apostle Paul said, "Be filled with the Spirit." He was not making a suggestion that this would be good for you only IF you feel the need. He was giving sound instructions for our benefit. But if you do not want to, that's ok, you can just stay as you are. Paul was stating that the Spirit-filled life is the will of God for everyone, and is essential for the fruitful Christian life.

Jesus commanded that we must be Spirit filled

You will observe in the next two biblical references that Jesus instructed His followers to stay in Jerusalem because they needed to be present for this great event. If this was not essential for their lives, Jesus would not have said if it was possible that they should stay.

"Behold, I send the Promise of My Father upon you; but tarry in the city of Jerusalem until you are endued with power from on high" (Luke 24:49).

And being assembled together with them, He commanded them not to depart from Jerusalem, but to wait for the promise of the Father, "which," He said:

> You have heard from Me; for John truly baptized with water, but you shall be baptized with the Holy Spirit not many days from now." Therefore, when they had come together, they asked Him, saying, "Lord, will You at this time restore the kingdom to Israel?" And He said to them, "It is not for you to know times or seasons which the Father has put in His own

authority. But you shall receive power when the Holy Spirit has come upon you; and you shall be witnesses to Me in Jerusalem, and in all Judea and Samaria, and to the end of the earth" (Acts 1:4-8).

We don't have to be geographically located in Jerusalem because the Holy Spirit has already been poured out. We don't have to tarry in the upper room, but we do have to get to a place where we receive Him. The same Holy Spirit that filled the hundred and twenty followers of Christ will fill your life. You may not experience the sound from heaven; you may not feel the force of the mighty rushing wind, and there may not be visible tongues of fire on your head. However, you will receive the same empowering from the same Holy Spirit.

"Which of you fathers, if your son asks for a fish, will give him a snake instead? Or if he asks for an egg, will give him a scorpion? If you then, though you are evil, know how to give good gifts to your children, how much more will your Father in heaven give the Holy Spirit to those who ask him!" (Luke 11:11-13, NIV).

The ministry of Jesus was empowered by the Spirit

This next section concerning the ministry of Jesus is essential to understand. Jesus was operating in the earth as a man who was filled, empowered and led by the Holy Spirit. Why is this so important? Jesus said that just as the Father had sent Him, in the same way, He is sending us. When we understand that Jesus was empowered and sent by God, then it makes sense that we are sent and empowered just like Jesus was. We could not do the works that Jesus did without the same Holy Spirit empowering our lives. For His followers to be given power and authority in the same way as Jesus, they had to stay in Jerusalem.

"...how God anointed Jesus of Nazareth with the Holy Spirit and with power, who went about doing good and healing all who were oppressed by the devil, for God was with Him." (Acts 10:38)

1. Filled with Spirit

Then Jesus came from Galilee to John at the Jordan to be baptized by him. And John tried to prevent Him, saying, "I need to be baptized by You, and are You coming to me?" But Jesus answered and said to him, "Permit it to be so now, for thus it is fitting for us to fulfill all righteousness." Then he allowed Him. When He had been baptized, Jesus came up immediately from the water; and behold, the heavens were opened to Him, and He saw the Spirit of God descending like a dove and alighting upon Him. And suddenly a voice came from heaven, saying, "This is My beloved Son, in whom I am well pleased" (Matthew 3:13-17).

2. Led by the Spirit and returned in power of the Spirit

"Then Jesus, being filled with the Holy Spirit, returned from the Jordan and was led by the Spirit into the wilderness" (Luke 4:1).

"Then Jesus returned in the power of the Spirit to Galilee, and news of Him went out through all the surrounding region. And He taught in their synagogues, being glorified by all" (Luke 4:14-15).

3. Began His ministry with this declaration

"The Spirit of the LORD is upon Me, Because He has anointed Me To preach the gospel to the poor; He has sent Me to heal the brokenhearted, To proclaim liberty to the captives And recovery of sight to the blind, To set at liberty those who are oppressed; To proclaim the acceptable year of the LORD" (Luke 4:18-19).

"Men of Israel, hear these words: Jesus of Nazareth, a Man attested by God to you by miracles, wonders, and signs which God did through Him in your midst, as you yourselves also know" (Acts 2:22).

Supernatural Boldness

It is important to understand that this courage that I am addressing is not the absence of fear, intimidation, and weakness. We will all face these things in varying degrees. However, we rise above our feelings of uncertainty, insecurity or inferiority and choose to stand in the boldness that is from God. We face our fears and feelings and declare that the greater One abides in us.

Feeling nervous in challenging situations is not necessarily a bad thing because we don't want to function in arrogance or self-confidence. Rather, we must have **GOD-confidence**.

BOLD

We overcome these feelings in the light of the revelation of who we are in Christ, in Him, we live and move and have our being (Acts 17:28). We understand that how we feel is subject to change but as new creations, we have not been given a spirit of fear but love, power and a sound mind. (2 Timothy 1:7)

To operate in the gifts of the Spirit, you have to possess God-given boldness; this is not arrogance. The boldness that I am addressing is cloaked in humility, grace, and meekness.

We are not robots, we are humans with feelings and emotions. To lack feelings and emotions is to be devoid of life. However, we cannot allow negative feelings of inadequacy to stop us from working for the glory of God. When God speaks to us, we have to deal with our thoughts, feelings, and emotions, especially when He requires us to do or say something that appears to be outrageous.

When I read certain passages of Scripture, I use my imagination and watch what takes place and how the circumstances affect the people involved. For example, in Acts 14:8-10, Paul is used by God to raise a cripple who had never walked:

> And in Lystra a certain man without strength in his feet was sitting, a cripple from his mother's womb, who had never walked. This man heard Paul speaking. Paul, observing him intently and seeing that he had faith to be healed, said with a loud voice, "Stand up

straight on your feet!" And he leaped and walked" (Acts 14:8-10).

In this account, I wonder what was going through Paul's mind. Paul recognized that the cripple had faith to be healed but I wonder if this great apostle had any doubts assailing his mind. I wonder if he was tempted not to speak, "Stand up straight on your feet!"? I wonder if Paul had total confidence or did he feel some insecurity in the event that the man would not be healed? Truth is, whenever God asks me to step out and say something like, "Stand up straight!" to a man who has never stood or walked, I feel a sense of panic, especially when the, "what if" thoughts grip my mind. What if he doesn't walk? What if he stands, and then collapses and has a heart attack from the stress?

I remember while working in South Africa, God told me to prophesy to a church that it would rain that very night. A severe drought had gripped the region, and God said that this would be broken. I had just watched the weather on TV, and I knew that there was no rain on the horizon, but I heard God's voice with crystal clarity. I obeyed God but with a deep sense of fear because I didn't want to be known as a false prophet.

What I'm saying may sound like a contradiction to being bold but bear with me. I spoke out what God told me and though I felt fear, I still did what God said to do—that's boldness! I may have felt deeply challenged by the possibility that the rain would not fall that night, but I obeyed God and not my feelings. Being bold is overriding your fears. Perhaps, when Paul saw the man's faith, he boldly spoke out, "Stand up straight!" However, he may have felt some trepidation prior. We don't know how he felt, but I do know that he was human and faced the same feelings we do today. It takes boldness to speak out strong words like, "Stand up straight!"

Ananias and Sapphira

To further show what being bold in the Spirit looks like, I want you to read about Ananias and Sapphira. While reading about their selfishness and lying to the Holy Spirit, I want you to notice in contrast to their weaknesses, the boldness of Peter.

> But a certain man named Ananias, with Sapphira his wife, sold a possession. And he kept back part of the proceeds, his wife also being aware of it, and brought a certain part and laid it at the apostles' feet. But Peter said, "Ananias, why has Satan filled your heart to lie to the Holy Spirit and keep back part of the price of the land for yourself? While it remained, was it not your own? And after it was sold, was it not in your own control? Why have you conceived this thing in your heart? You have not lied to men but to God." Then Ananias, hearing these words, fell down and breathed his last. So great fear came upon all those who heard these things. And the young men arose and wrapped him up, carried him out, and buried him. Now it was about three hours later when his wife came in, not

knowing what had happened. And Peter answered her, "Tell me whether you sold the land for so much?" She said, "Yes, for so much." Then Peter said to her, "How is it that you have agreed together to test the Spirit of the Lord? Look, the feet of those who have buried your husband are at the door, and they will carry you out." Then immediately she fell down at his feet and breathed her last. And the young men came in and found her dead, and carrying her out, buried her by her husband. So great fear came upon all the church and upon all who heard these things (Acts 5:1-11).

When I read this account of Peter exercising authority over this couple, I wonder what went through his mind, what he felt and how the situation affected him? There is no doubt that Peter was bold in the Spirit but how did he feel before and after this momentous day? Being bold in the Spirit does not remove feelings and emotions from us, but we rise above them and do what God instructs us to do.

Some years ago while living in South Africa, I led a Romanian gypsy family to the Lord. Up to that point, their families had been fortune tellers for generations. This conversion was a powerful experience for the family as the glory of God fell upon them sitting around the table in their trailer. Once we had regained some composure, I went to my car and got a Bible for each member of the family. As I presented them to the family the grandmother began to weep; she explained that she had never been to school and could not read or write, but she really wanted to read her new Bible.

Supernatural boldness gripped my heart. I laid my hands upon her eyes and with total confidence in God said to her, "Read, in Jesus' name!" I opened the Bible that was in her hands and said again, "Read!" Without hesitation, this precious grandmother began to read the passage of Scripture. We certainly celebrated the goodness of God that evening. To operate in the miraculous, you have to be bold.

Being bold is dependent on having a listening ear to the prompting of the Holy Spirit. You don't want to presumptuously step out and make declarations that are void of the manifestations of God. When people step out, and make bold and audacious statements that don't produce, it causes confusion for the recipients. They are left wondering if God cares about them or perhaps, they are left feeling that they are unworthy to be healed or touched by God. The Bible says that signs follow those who believe. When someone makes a declaration about what God is going to do, they had better have heard from God. He is not obliged to confirm someone's words when they are acting presumptuously or with insensitivity. Though I have used this verse already, I want to add it again, in order to support what I am saying:

"Men of Israel, hear these words: Jesus of Nazareth, a Man attested by God to you by miracles, wonders, and signs which God did through Him in your midst, as you yourselves also know" (Acts 2:22).

Notice that whenever Jesus spoke and acted in faith, God worked through Him. Jesus was sensitive to what the Father showed Him or said to Him. He did not just do His own thing but did the will of God. We can pray the prayer of faith over anyone and believe God for His touch upon the person's life but when we boldly command, "Get up and walk!" Make sure that you heard from God. Boldness is not an excuse to do your own thing or to act in a presumptuous way. We need to be sensitive to the Spirit of God and how He is leading us.

Peter and Simon the ex-sorcerer

In this account, you will learn that Peter was bold in the Spirit and used the power of God against this ex-fortune teller. Please be conscious of the reality that this apostolic judgment was not to bring Simon to a place of hopelessness but ultimately, for his rescue and salvation. Simon was just a young convert who was not even trained in the Word or developed in godly character. He was grossly insensitive to the realms of the Holy Spirit, and there seemed to be little tolerance for his indiscretion. This would be a defining moment for Simon. Either he would be freed, or he would stay in this lost state for the rest of his days.

And when Simon saw that through the laying on of the apostles' hands the Holy Spirit was given, he offered them money, saying, "Give me this power also, that anyone on whom I lay hands may receive the Holy Spirit." But Peter said to him, "Your money perish with you, because you thought that the gift of God could be purchased with money! You have neither part nor portion in this matter, for your heart is not right in the sight of God. Repent therefore of this your wickedness, and pray God if perhaps the thought of your heart may be forgiven you. For I see that you are poisoned by bitterness and bound by iniquity." Then Simon answered and said, "Pray to the Lord for me, that none of the things which you have spoken may come upon me." So when they had testified and preached the word of the Lord, they returned to Jerusalem, preaching the gospel in many villages of the Samaritans (Acts 8:18-25).

Peter made a swift decision and called down the word of the Lord against this ex-sorcerer. Notice the boldness and the discernment, "Your money perish with you, because you thought that the gift of God could be purchased with money! You have neither part nor portion in this matter, for your heart is not right in the sight of God" (Acts 8:20).

I arrived early for a Sunday meeting in a large church in South Florida. I had not met the pastor and wanted to spend a bit of time with him before ministering. I waited a while and eventually, one of the men ushered me into a prayer room to wait there. I prayed for about an hour and still had not met the pastor. I could hear the worship in the sanctuary, but I had not been invited in so I waited just praying in the spirit. Eventually, there was a knock at the door, and I was told that I was to go to the podium to preach. I was irritated by this as I still had not even spent ten seconds shaking the pastor's hand and introducing myself.

When I stood in front of the crowd of a thousand or more Sunday worshippers, I opened my address in this way: "A strange thing happened while waiting in the prayer room. I had a vision and saw a woman with two chains and collars coming from her left and right hand. Each collar was around two men's necks." Then I pointed to a woman on the front row and said, "You are the woman!" and to the man on her left and the one on the right I said, "You are the men!"

Then, I boldly began to address the woman, "You are the pastor's wife, and you control these two men." One of the men was the lead pastor and the other was the associate pastor. I then jumped from the stage to the floor and took authority of the spirit of Jezebel in the house and set her and the men free. Revival broke out and the church came into a great move of the Spirit. The point that I am trying to make is, I had to be bold, and though it is not how I typically greet a church, I had to do what God showed me.

Boldness in the Spirit is visible

Boldness in the Spirit will cause reaction from others:

1. They will be drawn to Jesus and will receive their miracle and deliverance.

2. They will seek to discredit and silence you.

"Now when they saw the boldness of Peter and John, and perceived that they were uneducated and untrained men, they marveled. And they realized that they had been with Jesus" (Acts 4:13).

The Church was birthed in Pentecost Power

The will of God is for all Christians to be Spirit filled (not just Spirit-indwelt but Spirit-empowered). Many Christians are backing away from the Spirit-filled life because of political correctness and salvation that avoids hell and makes heaven, but they don't want the passionate life of service that goes hand in hand with the grace that saves us.

Remember, the grace that saves us also calls us to the service of the King. While we are sons in our relationship with God, we are also servants of all humanity and the Church. The Holy Spirit empowers us for service. After the day of Pentecost, the fearing disciples became bold. The Holy Spirit is God—don't quench or grieve Him in your life. Rather seek His working in and through your life. It takes boldness to operate in miracles. The disciples in the face of persecution asked for boldness to speak and to flow in the power gifts (Acts 4:29-31). Today, like the disciples of old, we need the download of God's boldness upon our lives as we face an increasingly hostile society.

The bold Christian is:

- Passionate

- Abandoned

- Yielded

- Obedient to the Word and the will of God

- They have hearing ears and a surrendered will

Chapter 6

Bold in the Face of Persecution

According to Open Doors, a ministry serving the persecuted Christians worldwide, approximately three hundred and twenty-two Christians are killed every month. It is estimated that over seven hundred Christians suffer severe forms of violence (rape, beatings, abductions, arrests and forced marriages). Numerous churches and Christian-owned properties are destroyed. These atrocities take place against these Christians for one reason only—they are followers of Jesus Christ.

What is Christian Persecution?

Blessed are those who are persecuted for righteousness' sake, For theirs is the kingdom of heaven. "Blessed are you when they revile and persecute you, and say all kinds of evil against you falsely for My sake. Rejoice and be exceedingly glad, for great is your reward in heaven, for so they persecuted the prophets who were before you (Matthew 5:10-12).

Jesus warned His disciples that they, (and all subsequent followers of Jesus) would be persecuted. He also instructed the disciples what to do when facing persecution:

1. Outwardly, they are to rejoice.

2. Be exceedingly glad in their attitudes.

3. They were to feel honored rather than feel that somehow God had failed them.

4. Jesus would later exemplify to His disciples how to pray for their persecutors.

The Apostle Paul, who was a persecutor of the Church, said that all who live godly in Christ would face persecution (2 Timothy 3:12).

All the original Apostles, with the exception of John (Book of Revelation) died as martyrs. John could have died when cooked in a cauldron of hot oil, but he was spared and banished to Patmos. Later, he was released from Patmos and died at an old age of natural causes. Even the apostle Paul, who was a persecutor of the Church before his conversion was also eventually martyred. Throughout his Christian life and ministry, he faced constant persecution and suffering.

Persecution against Christians can be defined as any form of hostility towards them just because of their profession of faith in Christ. Persecution can be experienced in various ways:

- Verbal abuse
- Attitudes
- Discrimination
- Banishment from friends and family
- Loss of rights and protection

Christian community even in schools, colleges, and businesses. The pressure is building, and society is becoming increasingly intolerant of the Church.

Stephen is Martyred

When they heard these things they were cut to the heart, and they gnashed at him with their teeth. But he, being full of the Holy Spirit, gazed into heaven and saw the glory of God, and Jesus standing at the right hand of God, and said, "Look! I see the heavens opened and the Son of Man standing at the right hand of God!" Then they cried out with a loud voice, stopped their ears, and ran at him with one accord; and they cast him out of the city and stoned him. And the witnesses laid down their clothes at the feet of a young man named Saul. And they stoned Stephen as he was calling on God and saying, "Lord Jesus, receive my spirit." Then he knelt down and cried out with a loud voice, "Lord, do not charge them with this sin." And when he had said this, he fell asleep (Acts 7:54-60).

Stephen, the first Christian martyr was very bold in the face of barbaric persecution. Acts 1:8 says, "You shall receive power when the Holy Spirit has come upon you and you shall be my witnesses." The word "witnesses" is the Greek word, (martys). We get our English word "martyr" from this Greek word. When a believer is baptized in the Holy Spirit, he or she is empowered to share the Gospel even in the face of martyrdom or

- Physical violence

- Imprisonment

- Torture

- Death

The United States Department of State estimates that Christians face various forms of persecution in more than sixty countries. In forty-one of the fifty worst nations recognized for their persecution of Christians, Islamic extremists are the perpetrators. As the return of the Lord gets closer, it seems that persecution and resistance to the Church increases.

Boldness in the face of persecution is not just a subject for those working in Islamic nations but for many other countries around the world. Even in nations such as the USA, where we are guaranteed freedom to express our faith, there is open hostility. Christians are being threatened with hate speeches for making a stand on certain moral issues. Churches are struggling to acquire land and building permits are often only obtained after years of litigation. Liberal media attempts to discredit the Christian community as being people who are bigoted. Even the current POTUS (President Barak Obama) has been silent on extreme Islam but verbal about the so-called Right-Wing Christian Militia. If such a militia exists, I haven't seen any beheadings or crimes perpetrated against humanity by these "threats" to national security. I see increasing resistance to the suffering. A Spirit-filled follower of Jesus will be empowered to proclaim the Gospel even in an environment of hostility.

There are a few observations from this biblical account of the first Christian martyr that I would like to highlight:

1. Stephen was a deacon who served the widows and assisted the Apostles in the work of ministry.

2. He was highly anointed and operated in the power gifts of the Spirit.

3. The devil is more likely to target vessels of power who are actively engaged in the service of God. Those believers who are passive and who never access the realms of the anointing are less likely to be attacked. I am not saying that every person who is persecuted is on fire and sold out but the more prominent a person is in their Christian service, the more likely they are to be persecuted.

4. After Stephen's declaration of the Gospel, the Jewish people turned on him with venom. When I read this passage and the degree of hostility vented upon him, it appears that these persecutors were almost demonically inspired in their attack. I realize that some people who attack the Church are motivated by their religious zeal for their causes, such as radical

Muslims or Hindus. They believe that they are fighting for their god and his cause. Their god is a demonic spirit that operates in and through those in the captivity of the devil and is opposed to the advancement of the Gospel.

5. Saul was present at the stoning of Stephen giving approval to this act of hostility. I believe that when Stephen prayed and asked God to not lay this charge on his murderers, deep conviction came upon Saul. Later, Jesus said to Saul that it is hard to kick against the pricks. This was referring to the sharp stick farmers would use to direct an ox. Saul had been resistant to the prodding of the Holy Spirit. I believe that the Holy Spirit had convicted and prompted him to salvation through Christ even as the murder of Stephen took place.

6. The most outstanding observation from this first martyr was his boldness in the face of hostility. He was poised, dignified, and he displayed no sign of terror. He was bold!

Peter and John were threatened

This story begins when Peter and John healed a lame man at the Gate called Beautiful. The people's excitement at this outstanding miracle caused a multitude to gather and after Peter had delivered a passionate presentation of the Gospel, over five thousand men received Jesus as Lord of their lives. The religious leaders in the city were visibly shaken by the event and at the overwhelmingly positive response from the people. The Sanhedrin believed that their popularity had shifted, and their only option to stay in power was to stop the disciples from propagating their message about Jesus.

A point that should be noted concerning the Sanhedrin is that this was the same council that had sentenced Jesus to death. These were not true spiritual leaders who were concerned about the Word of God, they were insecure men who were more concerned that their power would be threatened by this growing movement of Jesus followers. They arrested Peter and John and after their meeting tried to prevent the disciples from preaching their message that salvation is found in no other name than Jesus. The disciples boldly faced their judges and refused to comply. It should be noted that the boldness of Peter and John was visible to this council.

"Now when they saw the boldness of Peter and John, and perceived that they were uneducated and untrained men, they marveled. And they realized that they had been with Jesus" (Acts 4:13).

Peter and John were bold in a number of areas:

1. They were bold in the Spirit when they operated in the power of God.

2. They were bold in the Gospel when they shared at Pentecost and also as they preached on this occasion. The response to the message was

enormous, and thousands of souls were swept into the Kingdom and joined the Church.

3. They were bold in facing their opponents and spoke with conviction concerning the death and resurrection of Jesus; as well as their role in propelling this new movement forward. They were not intimidated by the rulers and elders neither were they rude or arrogant. I like to think of them as respectfully bold.

4. They prayed with boldness for more boldness.

"Now, Lord, look on their threats, and grant to Your servants that with all boldness they may speak Your word, by stretching out Your hand to heal, and that signs and wonders may be done through the name of Your holy Servant Jesus" (Acts 4:29-30).

When they were freed, Peter and John met with their companions, and they began to passionately pray concerning the building resentment against the Church and the looming persecution. These disciples did not pray for protection or deliverance, but they prayed for increased boldness to preach the Gospel and increased manifestations of God's power (Acts 4:23-31). There was no Red Cross or Amnesty International; there were no agencies that protected religious rights. The disciples had to pray and get help from God. The help they desired was not safety but the ability and anointing to increase the effectiveness of their ministry. This is what we need in the growing hostile society. Not protection but supernatural manifestations of God. The anointing of God on our lives may not protect us from persecution, but it will cause our impact to be felt in a significant way.

The Persecutor became the Persecuted

The Apostle Paul faced years of persecution and suffering for the sake of the Gospel. There are many scriptures that discuss his multiple sufferings and imprisonments. In this chapter, I will discuss just a few. Pauls' first attempt to preach the Gospel just days after his Damascus Road conversion ended with him being lowered over the city wall in a basket to avoid death.

> Immediately, he preached the Christ in the synagogues, that He is the Son of God. Then all who heard were amazed, and said, "Is this not he who destroyed those who called on this name in Jerusalem, and has come here for that purpose, so that he might bring them bound to the chief priests?" But Saul increased all the more in strength, and confounded the Jews who dwelt in Damascus, proving that this Jesus is the Christ. Now after many days were past, the Jews plotted to kill him. But their plot became known to Saul. And they watched the gates day and night, to kill him. Then the disciples took him by night and let him down through the wall in a large basket (Acts 9:20-25).

After this first encounter where the persecutor became the persecuted, Paul would face years of violent abuse because of his love for Jesus. The devil would harass

Paul's ministry with one goal to silence the Gospel and to limit the sphere of his influence. This is clearly made known in Acts 13:49-50. The Word of the Lord was spreading throughout the region: "And the word of the Lord was being spread throughout all the region. But the Jews stirred up the devout and prominent women and the chief men of the city, raised up persecution against Paul and Barnabas, and expelled them from their region" (Acts 13:49-50).

Whenever the Word starts to spread, the devil will use people to stop the impact. In this case, he chose prominent women and the chief men of the city. Demonic spirits are behind the people who are stirring up trouble for the Church. These people were not even aware of the strategy of the devil; they thought they were doing the right thing, but they were, in fact, opposing the Lord of glory. We have to understand that behind the people who are causing trouble are demonic spirits. Remember, we are not wrestling against flesh and blood (Ephesians 6:12). If the devil can't mute the sound of the Gospel, he will see to it that you are expelled; he did this to Paul and Barnabas. Remember, his strategies never change. Be on the alert and be bold, remember the greater One lives in you. No weapon formed against you can prosper (Isaiah 54:17).

Now it happened in Iconium that they went together to the synagogue of the Jews, and so spoke that a great multitude both of the Jews and of the Greeks believed. But the unbelieving Jews stirred up the Gentiles and poisoned their minds against the brethren. Therefore, they stayed there a long time, speaking boldly in the Lord, who was bearing witness to the word of His grace, granting signs and wonders to be done by their hands. But the multitude of the city was divided: part sided with the Jews, and part with the apostles. And when a violent attempt was made by both the Gentiles and Jews, with their rulers, to abuse and stone them, they became aware of it and fled to Lystra and Derbe, cities of Lycaonia, and to the surrounding region (Acts 14:1-6).

As the Apostles were speaking boldly and the multitudes were responding to the message of life, the enemy of the Church was also busy. Though the devil is invisible, he is at work to counteract the progress of the Gospel. He will use people to be his vehicle to stop the work of God. Persecution is his most common method of hampering the work of God, and at times, violent and vicious cruelty against the servants of God.

Then Jews from Antioch and Iconium came there; and having persuaded the multitudes, they stoned Paul and dragged him out of the city, supposing him to be dead. However, when the disciples gathered around him, he rose up and went into the city. And the next day he departed with Barnabas to Derbe (Acts 14:19-20).

In this incident, the Jews attacked Paul and viciously stoned him, but God preserved and raised him. There are times when people die as martyrs but in this account, God kept Paul alive; it was not the time of his departure.

Paul and Silas were cruelly beaten and imprisoned, not because they did anything wrong but because they did a good work for the glory of God. They cast a demon out of a young girl who operated in a spirit of divination, and instead of being applauded and thanked for their service to God, they were beaten and placed in prison. They were not criminals but committed apostles carrying the Gospel flame.

> Then the multitude rose up together against them, and the magistrates tore off their clothes and commanded them to be beaten with rods. And when they had laid many stripes on them, they threw them into prison, commanding the jailer to keep them securely. Having received such a charge, he put them into the inner prison and fastened their feet in the stocks (Acts 16:22-24).

Again, God delivered them from their stocks and the prison through a miraculous shaking that took place. In this case, God intervened and delivered Paul and Silas from the prison. They had worshiped and prayed and at the midnight hour, God broke through for them. The consequence of their deliverance is that the jailer and his household (of believing adults) were saved.

On a side note of interest—Paul had received the "Macedonian Call," He and Silas were right in the center of God's will when they were beaten and thrown in jail.

They had obeyed God and traveled there by inspiration from Him. Sometimes, when we are doing the explicit will of God, we are attacked through persecution. Some people may feel that when you are doing the will of God and obeying God that you will have divine protection and no evil will take place. On the contrary, it's not so when it comes to persecution; this is not God letting you down or not protecting you. This is the glory of suffering for the sake of the Word and doing the will of God. Remember what Jesus said concerning persecution. I quoted this earlier in this chapter but it's worth repeating:

> Blessed are those who are persecuted for righteousness' sake, For theirs is the kingdom of heaven. "Blessed are you when they revile and persecute you, and say all kinds of evil against you falsely for My sake. Rejoice and be exceedingly glad, for great is your reward in heaven, for so they persecuted the prophets who were before you" (Matthew 5:10-12).

Paul and Silas were protected and delivered from the prison but only after the beatings and the abuse. Paul would eventually be killed. When it came time for his departure, and he had run his race, he was a partaker of the glory of dying as a martyr.

The Christians in Smyrna were encouraged and warned that they would be persecuted

"Do not fear any of those things which you are about to suffer. Indeed, the devil is about to throw some of you into prison, that you may be tested, and you will have tribulation ten days. Be faithful until death, and I will give you the crown of life" (Revelation 2:10).

Peter was delivered from prison

I enjoy studying history, and I especially appreciate being able to visit places where Biblical events took place. I once went to Corinth and stood at the ruins where Paul stayed. I also visited the house of Peter, on the shores of Galilee. I preached a short sermon on Mars Hill where Paul reasoned with the ancient philosophers. In my travels, I have been to Rome a few times and visited ancient Rome on every occasion.

On one trip to Rome, I visited the Carcere Mamertino (Italian) or the Mamertine Prison overlooking the ruins of the Roman Forum. It was not built like modern prisons as we know them today, it was a dungeon. Prisoners were lowered about 12 feet down through a hole in an underground cell. The dimensions of the cell measured about 6.5 feet (2 meters) high, 30 feet (9 meters) long and 22 feet (6.7 meters) wide.

I imagined the deplorable conditions, the stench of human waste, filth, and darkness in those cells where both the Apostles Paul and Peter waited for their death sentences to be carried out. These two Bible heroes deserved to be honored and cared for, but their honor was not retirement on a private estate—a place where they could write their memoirs. No! It was a stinking dark hole in the sewers of Rome.

I spent some time praying in the dungeon and asked God to make me a man who serves the Church like they did, in a way that they did. I also allowed my analytical mind to wander a bit. I considered Paul and Silas being delivered from the prison in Philippi, but Paul would die in Rome and spend his last days in the place where I was standing. There would be no earthquake and chains falling off, and no way out with angels opening locks. There would be no last-minute reprieve. He would be unceremoniously hauled out of the hole in the ground, and be put to death.

Eusebius, an early church historian, wrote that Paul was beheaded soon after the fire that razed Rome. He was not crucified because he was a Roman citizen. I marveled at the courage and boldness in his heart. Here is what Paul had to say concerning his impending death:

> For I am already being poured out as a drink offering, and the time of my departure is at hand. I have fought the good fight, I have finished the race, I have kept the faith. Finally, there is laid up for me the crown of righteousness, which the Lord, the righteous Judge, will give to me on that Day, and not to me only but also to all who have loved His appearing (2 Timothy 4:6-8).

Paul lived his life sacrificially, a living sacrifice (Romans 12:1), a life poured out as a drink offering (2 Timothy

4:6) and with a constant sentence of death upon his life (2 Corinthians 1:9). Paul was bold in the face of suffering and death.

In Acts 12, we read about Peter's deliverance from jail. The Church prayed all night, yet, he would, after years of loyal service—be crucified. There would be no angel waking him, and leading him out of a locked cell. There would be no all-night prayer meeting and answered prayer. Tradition says that he was led to the inverted cross and died as a martyr. (Peter requested, to die this way saying that he was not worthy to die in the same position that Jesus died). Jesus had warned Peter that he would one day die as a martyr.

> Most assuredly, I say to you, when you were younger, you girded yourself and walked where you wished; but when you are old, you will stretch out your hands, and another will gird you and carry you where you do not wish." This He spoke, signifying by what death he would glorify God. And when He had spoken this, He said to him, "Follow Me" (John 21:18-19)

In Acts 12, we not only read about Peter's deliverance from persecution, but we also read about the first Apostle to be martyred. Peter lived but his friend James died.

> Now about that time Herod the king stretched out his hand to harass some from the church. Then he killed James the brother of John with the sword. And because he saw that it pleased the Jews, he proceeded

further to seize Peter also. Now it was during the Days of Unleavened Bread (Acts 12:1-3).

James and his brother John

The wicked king, Herod Agrippa was the grandson of the murderer of all the children of Bethlehem who were slaughtered at the time of the birth of Jesus. King Agrippa was the nephew of Herod Antipas who had John the Baptist beheaded. He called for the killing of James (the brother of John) and the arrest of Peter.

We learn about James and John, the two brothers whose mother requested a special place for them beside Jesus.

> Then the mother of Zebedee's sons came to Him with her sons, kneeling down and asking something from Him. And He said to her, "What do you wish?" She said to Him, "Grant that these two sons of mine may sit, one on Your right hand and the other on the left, in Your kingdom." But Jesus answered and said, "You do not know what you ask. Are you able to drink the cup that I am about to drink, and be baptized with the baptism that I am baptized with?" They said to Him, "We are able." So He said to them, "You will indeed drink My cup, and be baptized with the baptism that I am baptized with; but to sit on My right hand and on My left is not Mine to give, but it is for those for whom it is prepared by My Father" (Matthew 20:20-23).

Jesus had just spoken about this death and resurrection. Though he had mentioned this a few times, the reality had not penetrated the minds of the disciples. (Matthew 16;21; Matthew 17:22 and now Matthew 20:18-19). The mother of James and John was with the disciples and right after Jesus spoke about His death, she requested a place next to His throne. Talk about insensitivity! Jesus then replied with a prophetic challenge for both her sons, "Are you able to drink of the cup of my suffering and are you able to be baptized in my suffering?" Both James and John would later partake of that cup and baptism. James would be the first Apostle martyred and John would be boiled in a cauldron of hot oil. Though he did not die, he was banished to Patmos. As previously stated, John suffered persecution, but he died of natural causes.

You may recall the thirty Ethiopian Christians who were martyred by ISIS in Libya. They were unceremoniously paraded in their orange jumpsuits and later shot and beheaded by their gloating killers. The world was horrified and angered by this act of terror on innocent victims. Many Christians are being killed in various nations but the countries where Christians are killed, tortured and imprisoned the most are North Korea, Iraq, Iran, Syria, India, and Pakistan. What should be our Christian response to these violent or subtle persecutors?

All religions and cults suffer at the hands of ignorant people. Mormons are treated unkindly; Jehovah Witnesses were severely persecuted in the past and still today, they face harsh treatment. Witches were burnt at the stake, and Hindus attacked Muslims and vice versa. Jews were exterminated and in many places, there is still strong anti-Semitic sentiments expressed. However, Christians have been persecuted from the inception of Christianity to this day and the devil has used persecution to limit the advancement of the Gospel.

What we have to remember is that we are not of this world; we may live in this world but as born again believers, we are different. We are not conformed to this world's way of doing and saying things. Instead, we have a Kingdom response to what life and circumstances bring our way. We are shaped by what the Word of God says rather than what our culture says, the media and even what those who are near and dear to us have to say. We have a higher allegiance to our God for we are citizens of heaven. We are a holy people, a royal priesthood and members of God's household.

In the light of persecution, we see how Jesus treated those who abused, tortured, and crucified Him. He forgave them and showed no fear. He was like a sheep led to the slaughter. He even had time to welcome into His kingdom the one thief who was crucified next to Him. He had words of compassion for His mother and those weeping with her. Oh, what a marvelous Savior! He exemplified boldness, dignity, and grace. We see the same attitude demonstrated in Stephen as his persecutors stoned him to death.

BOLD

To summarize our response to persecution:

- We are to be bold

- We are to be brave and strong

- We are to forgive our persecutors

- We are to pray for our enemies

- We are to rejoice and be exceedingly glad

- If we die, we do so in glory and if we live, we press on and keep doing the will of God

- If we live, we pray and ask God to fill us with the Spirit that we may be bolder and more anointed

Chapter 7

Bold in Spiritual Warfare

Spiritual Foes Exist

Do you know that many pastors don't believe that the devil is real? If some pastors don't teach about the reality of the devil, then how will the people be able to stand against a foe that they don't believe exists?

"There are two equal and opposite errors we can fall into concerning demons: One is to disbelieve in their existence. The other is to believe, and to feel an excessive and unhealthy interest in them. They themselves are equally pleased with both error" C.S. Lewis.

When I was a brand new believer, I had no idea that the devil or demons were real. I thought the realm of the devil was imaginary or folklore. I believed that these supposed creatures were much like adult fairy tales except, they were on the dark side. The precious couple who discipled me, Arthur and Phyllis Morris, one day began to describe the realms of the demonic and dark forces that are at work. This teaching freaked me out! I was like the kids in the Monsters Inc. movie.

Before I discovered the authority of the name of Jesus and the Christian armor, I felt very exposed to the realms of darkness. When I found out about the reality of the demonic realms, it made the scripture, "Watch and pray" very real (Matthew 26:41). I would keep my eyes open when I prayed just in case one of these dark forces tried to penetrate my life.

One night, I forgot to watch—keep my eyes open, and pray. I prayed with my eyes closed. Suddenly, claws ripped into my back, (I had no shirt on), and I screamed, "In the name of Jesus!" I was kneeling in prayer and as I stood up rebuking the devil, my little kitten who was using my back as a scratch pad went flying through the air. From that day on, the kitten would hiss at me and arch its back. I wanted to rename my kitten, "Satan."

The devil and his dark cohorts are real. They are not myths or legends; they are creatures that do exist in the unseen realms around us. Paul gave clear instruction concerning spiritual warfare.

Finally, my brethren, be strong in the Lord and in the power of His might. Put on the whole armor of God, that you may be able to stand against the wiles of the devil. For we do not wrestle against flesh and blood, but against principalities, against powers, against the rulers of the darkness of this age, against spiritual hosts of wickedness in the heavenly places (Ephesians 6:10-12).

Here is a list of the enemies that oppose the Church and our lives as followers of Jesus:

- The Devil
- Principalities

- Powers

- Rulers of the darkness

- Spiritual hosts of wickedness

- Demons

We should not be governed by or be afraid of our enemies—we must be bold. Our spiritual weapons are mighty in God; with this armament, we can wage a successful warfare. God has not given us inferior weaponry to fight an enemy that we cannot see. As you read the context of the passage that discusses our spiritual weapons, you will notice the contrast between the humility and boldness found in Paul's ministry. In his relationship with fellow Christians, he was meek and gentle. To those, (false teachers, the one's who were the instruments of the devil, who wanted to cause trouble) he was bold. He was also bold against the devil and his forces. Paul realized that he was dealing with three specific groups:

1. The victims—the innocent, trusting lambs.

2. The perpetrators—the false teachers or those who were destabilizing the Church.

3. The enemy—the spiritual powers at work using people to accomplish their strategy to overpower the Church.

Now I, Paul, myself am pleading with you by the meekness and gentleness of Christ--who in presence am lowly among you, but being absent am bold toward you. But I beg you that when I am present I may not be bold with that confidence by which I intend to be bold against some, who think of us as if we walked according to the flesh. For though we walk in the flesh, we do not war according to the flesh. For the weapons of our warfare are not carnal but mighty in God for pulling down strongholds, casting down arguments and every high thing that exalts itself against the knowledge of God, bringing every thought into captivity to the obedience of Christ, and being ready to punish all disobedience when your obedience is fulfilled (2 Corinthians 10:1-6).

We can be bold in spiritual warfare against the forces who wage war against our lives and the Church because Jesus has given us spiritual weapons that are mighty. We have been given armor to protect us (Ephesians 6:12-17); as well as weapons that are powerful to wage a warfare. Here is a list of our fighting weapons:

- The sword of the Spirit which is the Word of God (Ephesians 6:17).

- The Name of Jesus (Mark 16:17).

- The Blood of Jesus (Revelation 12:11).

- The power of prayer and intercession (Ephesians 6:10 -17).

We have a protection that comes from God; this God-given protection is far superior to the enemy's attacks. Though we don't have to be afraid of these enemies, we must be on the alert as they are on the prowl seeking to gain an advantage over us.

"Be sober, be vigilant; because your adversary the devil walks about like a roaring lion, seeking whom he may devour. Resist him, steadfast in the faith, knowing that the same sufferings are experienced by your brotherhood in the world" (1 Peter 5:8-9).

The reason we are bold in the spiritual realm against these enemies is that the Lord is on our side (Romans 8:31) and with His authority, we are more than conquerors (Romans 8:37). The greater One lives in us (1 John 4:4).

Men, we are at war!

After months of training as infantrymen, we were assembled and the general who had come to address us said this, "Men we are at war! You will be mobilized into the operational area tonight, and by tomorrow, you will be in combat." As soldiers, we were not trained to march on parade grounds and stay in a base—we were trained to fight.

Just like the general said to us, so many years ago, I want to say to you, "Men, we are at war!" There is a spiritual war that is being fought in the unseen realm. Some Christians are oblivious to the realm of the spirit; they are so caught up in the affairs of everyday life that they don't even realize what is taking place. On the other hand, not every situation that we face is demonically inspired. Some issues that we face are just storms of life that come to all people. There are some things that go wrong because we make a wrong decision, we can do or say something that comes back to bite us. These things cannot be attributed to the devil but are solely caused by our actions.

It would be nice if we could blame the devil for everything but in some cases, things just don't work out like we hoped. There are some sicknesses that can be demonic (known as a spirit of infirmity) and then there are some sicknesses that exist because we live in a fallen world. Not everything that comes against us is demonic. However, some troubles that we face are strategies from the realms of the demons.

We are given the gift of discernment of spirits to address the situation accurately. Paul was hindered by Satan (1 Thessalonians 2:18). He was buffeted in his flesh; he called it a thorn in his side (2 Corinthians 12:7). Satan wanted to sift Peter like wheat; in other words, the devil wanted to take him down (Luke 22:31).

We are at war! The devil, though defeated and stripped of power is unrelenting in his strategies to hinder our lives from fruitful service. He is constantly at work to bring division in the churches and to discredit ministries. He is a liar who works through deception and is a master at causing confusion. He will use every disruptive technique in his arsenal to stop our growth from taking place. We are told not to be ignorant of his schemes, but alas, many are oblivious and so he is constantly at work to destroy all that God wants to accomplish.

Fight the Good Fight of Faith

"Fight the good fight of faith, lay hold on eternal life, to which you were also called and have confessed the good confession in the presence of many witnesses" (1 Timothy 6:12).

We are called to fight the good fight of faith:

- A good fight is one where we win

- A good fight is a fight where the enemy is guaranteed to lose

It is a fight of faith. That means feelings or sight don't count; all that is important is faith to win because Jesus has won. No demon, principality or power is stronger than the name of Jesus. When we have done all, we stand. We stand strong or bold in the Lord as more than a conqueror.

Deliverance

While dealing with the subject of being bold in spiritual warfare, I want to deal briefly with casting out demons. This is an important aspect of the New Testament ministry given to us by Jesus. In the ministry of deliverance, we engage against spiritual forces and bring God's redemption to those lives that are in the chains of demonic bondage. We need boldness to stand in the place of divine authority and cast out demons.

Over the years of ministry, I have found that many Christians become almost paralyzed with fear when in a place where demons start manifesting. This fear that manifests is the product of their ignorance.

If these fearful Christians knew the following, they would rise in boldness:

1. If they grasped their identity of who they are in Christ.

2. If they understood the divine authority that they have been given by Jesus.

3. If they only knew the power of God that resides within their lives.

"Pastor...Pastor, please come quickly, there are demons manifesting in my home; I don't know what to do!"

As a pastor, I have received multiple calls to come quickly to the homes of members who were praying for their family or friends and demons started manifesting. To bring this into perspective, I have taught in my churches that we have authority to cast out demons. I have had multiple demonic manifestations in meetings when praying for people so the members have had deliverance demonstrated. However, when the demons manifest, they forget what was taught and what they had seen— and fear takes over.

As a missionary working in the villages of Africa and later in India, I have been in numerous meetings where demons have manifested. I have cast them out and set hundreds of lives free. I am bold in this realm because I know the reality of my authority in Christ. I could write a book that describes my experiences on the subject of violent manifestations of demons.

I have faced these vile creatures trying to attack me in meetings, but I have stood in the boldness of God and brought deliverance to the lives of many. In some encounters, I have seen these demons moving like serpents in the bellies, throats, and extremities of people. I have seen these demons attempt to throttle their victims and harm them; but I have stood in the place of divine commission and said, "In the name of Jesus, come out and return no more!" I have watched as these demons flee their victims and I have experienced how the delivered person smiles, laughs and is filled with the Spirit. I have seen the joy that floods their souls as they come into real freedom. Oh, what joy when we can say, "Who the Son sets free is free indeed!"

Jesus casts out demons

"When evening had come, they brought to Him many who were demon-possessed. And He cast out the spirits with a word, and healed all who were sick" (Matthew 8:16).

The ministry of Jesus was prolific when it came to casting out demons. As you read through the Gospels, there are a number of occasions where Jesus brought freedom to people who were demonized. In fact, His ministry was criticized, and He was accused of casting out demons by the power of Beelzebub (Matthew 12:24). Jesus was also known for being filled with the Spirit and a part of His ministry was setting the captives free (Acts 10:38; Luke 4:18-19).

"How God anointed Jesus of Nazareth with the Holy Spirit and with power, who went about doing good and healing all who were oppressed by the devil, for God was with Him" (Acts 10:38).

"The Spirit of the LORD is upon Me, Because He has anointed Me To preach the gospel to the poor; He has sent Me to heal the brokenhearted, To proclaim liberty to the captives And recovery of sight to the blind, To set at liberty those who are oppressed; To proclaim the acceptable year of the LORD" (Luke 4:18-19).

The ministry of Jesus was focused on a few areas:

1. He came to seek and to save the lost.

2. He came to die for our sins.

3. He taught and trained His disciples; they would become the continuum of His ministry.

4. He came to demonstrate the Kingdom with power, casting out demons, healing the sick, and working miracles.

But if I cast out demons with the finger of God, surely the kingdom of God has come upon you. When a strong man, fully armed, guards his own palace, his goods are in peace. But when a stronger than he comes upon him and overcomes him, he takes from him all his armor in which he trusted, and divides his spoils (Luke 11:20-22).

Jesus gave His disciples authority to cast out demons. Every commission that He gave to His followers included the authority to expel demons. The twelve disciples whom Jesus was training to be the apostles early in their preparation would be given the power to cast out demons.

"And when He had called His twelve disciples to Him, He gave them power over unclean spirits, to cast them out, and to heal all kinds of sickness and all kinds of disease" (Matthew 10:1).

"And as you go, preach, saying, 'The kingdom of heaven is at hand.' Heal the sick, cleanse the lepers, raise the dead, cast out demons. Freely you have received, freely give" (Matthew 10:7-8).

In the same way, Jesus gave authority to the seventy disciples to heal the sick and cast out demons. When they returned, they were excited because they had cast out demons.

> Then the seventy returned with joy, saying, "Lord, even the demons are subject to us in Your name." And He said to them, "I saw Satan fall like lightning from heaven. Behold, I give you the authority to trample on serpents and scorpions, and over all the power of the enemy, and nothing shall by any means hurt you. Nevertheless, do not rejoice in this, that the spirits are subject to you, but rather rejoice because your names are written in heaven" (Luke 10:17-20).

Jesus gave them some basic instructions to keep things in perspective. He gave a quick lesson to His zealous disciples reminding them that their celebration should be in the fact that they are citizens of heaven and saved.

The Great Commission included the authority to cast out demons

> "And these signs will follow those who believe: In My name they will cast out demons; they will speak with new tongues; they will take up serpents; and if they drink anything deadly, it will by no means hurt them; they will lay hands on the sick, and they will recover" (Mark 16:17-18).

Philip casts out demons

> Therefore, those who were scattered went everywhere preaching the word. Then Philip went down to the city of Samaria and preached Christ to them. And the

multitudes with one accord heeded the things spoken by Philip, hearing and seeing the miracles which he did. For unclean spirits, crying with a loud voice, came out of many who were possessed; and many who were paralyzed and lame were healed. And there was great joy in that city. (Acts 8:4-8)

Paul casts out demons

Now it happened, as we went to prayer, that a certain slave girl possessed with a spirit of divination met us, who brought her masters much profit by fortune-telling. This girl followed Paul and us, and cried out, saying, "These men are the servants of the Most High God, who proclaim to us the way of salvation." And this she did for many days. But Paul, greatly annoyed, turned and said to the spirit, "I command you in the name of Jesus Christ to come out of her." And he came out that very hour (Acts 16:16-18).

"Now God worked unusual miracles by the hands of Paul, so that even handkerchiefs or aprons were brought from his body to the sick, and the diseases left them and the evil spirits went out of them" (Acts 19:11-12).

Other Apostles cast out demons

"Also a multitude gathered from the surrounding cities to Jerusalem, bringing sick people and those who were tormented by unclean spirits, and they were all healed" (Acts 5:16).

We have seen that Jesus boldly cast out demons, His disciples were also bold—they set people free from demonic control. Throughout the ages, men and women of God have perpetuated the ministry of deliverance. With boldness, this generation of Christians must continue the ministry of authority that brings deliverance to the captives.

Preaching the Gospel

When we boldly preach the Gospel we are engaging in spiritual warfare. We are breaking the vice-like grip that the devil has on the lives of people. When a person is unsaved, they are led and controlled by the devil. I know that this statement can freak people out, but I am just quoting the Scriptures. This does not mean that every unsaved person is demonized. What it does mean is that all unsaved people are in the grip of Satan.

And you He made alive, who were dead in trespasses and sins, in which you once walked according to the course of this world, according to the prince of the power of the air, the spirit who now works in the sons of disobedience, among whom also we all once conducted ourselves in the lusts of our flesh, fulfilling the desires of the flesh and of the mind, and were by nature children of wrath, just as the others (Ephesians 2:1-3).

In Acts 26:18, (this is the Red letter edition, in other words, Jesus said these words to Paul). When the Gospel is preached, people will have their eyes opened; they will turn from darkness to light and from the power of Satan to God. Every person who is unsaved is under the control of Satan.

"To open their eyes, in order to turn them from darkness to light, and from the power of Satan to God, that they may receive forgiveness of sins and an inheritance among those who are sanctified by faith in Me" (Acts 26:18).

The good news is a life-transforming message that liberates lives from darkness and from the grip of Satan. The Bible declares that with our Christian armor, our feet are shod with the sandals of the Gospel of peace. When we put our feet down, we are taking the ground from Satan and bringing liberation to the lives of men and women.

"Behold, I give you the authority to trample on serpents and scorpions, and over all the power of the enemy, and nothing shall by any means hurt you" (Luke 10:19).

Prayer is Engaging in Spiritual Warfare

When I was a young pastor, I would spend hours engaging in focused prayer on the spiritual forces of darkness. Though I'm now a little older, I still pray for a few hours daily, but I no longer focus on what the devil is doing—I focus on the God solution.

Let me explain—I used to spend most of my prayer time binding, loosing, casting out, and tearing down. For my zeal, I'd get 100% but for results, not much. I'll never forget the day when the Lord spoke clearly to me. I was in my prayer room, shouting, resisting with all my might against the principalities and powers, when suddenly in the midst of my fervent activity, I heard with crystal clarity the voice of the Head of the Church, my Boss, and Friend. He said to me, "Who is your prayer time directed towards?" He went on to say that He didn't share the throne room with the devil. I quickly took account of my prayers and realized that though I would start off speaking to God, in the next breath, I would be confronting all of hell.

"For this reason I bow my knees to the Father of our Lord Jesus Christ" (Ephesians 3:14).

This verse has illuminated my spirit because I became aware that most of my prayer time was spent rebuking the devil. The only value in all this time of prayer was for my soul, as I felt that I had fulfilled my duty in this holy war. This was a turning point in my prayer life, and from then on, I would direct my love, adoration, and prayers to God.

Now, we are left with the question of what to do with the scriptures about fighting the devil, such as "We wrestle against the enemy" (Ephesians 6:12). How do I wrestle against the enemy? The answer is found in the following scriptures:

"Finally, my brethren, be strong in the Lord and in the power of His might. Put on the whole armor of God, that you may be able to stand against the wiles of the devil" (Ephesians 6:10).

We assume the posture of spiritual authority and in our attitude, we see ourselves as strong in the Lord. Remember, our strength is in the Lord; this is a supernatural strength and boldness. We obtain this boldness by faith. Even though we may feel weak, we declare, "I am strong!" With this attitude, we take up position in prayer.

> And take the helmet of salvation, and the sword of the Spirit, which is the word of God; praying always with all prayer and supplication in the Spirit, being watchful to this end with all perseverance and supplication for all the saints—and for me, that utterance may be given to me, that I may open my mouth boldly to make known the mystery of the gospel, for which I am an ambassador in chains; that in it I may speak boldly, as I ought to speak (Ephesians 6:10-11, 17-20).

Often quoted is the passage of scripture about Daniel who fought the prince of Persia (Daniel 10:10-21).

- Daniel had received prophetic revelation regarding the Last Days (v. 1)

- Daniel fasted and prayed for three full weeks (vv. 2-3)

- Daniel received a holy visitation. Note the similarities between Daniel's visitation and John's in Revelation (vv. 4-9)

Daniel was engaged in a spiritual conflict for twenty-one days against the prince of Persia. Note that in this time, Daniel prayed and fasted (vv. 12-15). Though locked in holy warfare in his spirit so that he could obtain revelation, he was not in a "shouting match" with the devil but in deep prayer. It is true that there are principalities and ruling spirits and at times, we are brought into conflict against them. This battle is fought and won on our knees before God. He dispatches strong angels to fight on our behalf. Our prayers make a difference in the spiritual atmosphere and as a result, changes take place in the natural realm.

We need to be bold in spiritual warfare through the power of prayer. When we pray and seek the will of God, we are engaging in powerful spiritual warfare.

Taking Authority

A while back, I traveled to conduct meetings in Togo, West Africa. This country is renowned for the dark practices of voodoo, and this trip was one of the most challenging ever. The positives were that the meetings were very fruitful with many people being saved, healed, and delivered from demonic spirits.

The negatives of this mission were that everything went wrong that could go wrong. The vehicle broke down on various occasions and caused me to be significantly late for some meetings. The plane broke down, and I sat on the runway in the middle of the Sahara Desert for hours with no air conditioning.

The BO on that flight was nauseating with the high temperatures and obviously, the people didn't use deodorant or anti-perspirant. I got in late that evening and went straight into the stadium meeting. They gave me the microphone and said, we left the bad cases for you. So I got to pray for the blind, lame, and deaf after twenty hours of flying, no food, and high temperatures. Thank God He showed up, and we had a few miracles.

One night, a demon manifested in my room and tried to choke me. The presence of evil was tangible and though this was not the first time such an attack had taken place; this was the strongest attempt upon my life. By the time I could gather myself and whisper the name of Jesus, this dark presence of ultimate darkness was broken. I lay on my bed with the ceiling fan rotating above my head and worshiped God. The sweet presence of the Lord filled the room; He strengthened and encouraged me.

The next day my meeting was invaded by at least a dozen voodoo witch doctors. The ringleaders kept throwing curses on my translators, and they were being struck dumb. I shouted with the loud shout of the Lord and the witch doctors went running and screaming out of the meetings, except the ringleader who kept trying to disturb me.

She came forward and requested prayer. The power of God hit her, and she fell to the ground. She stood up and asked for more prayer—again the power of God threw her to the floor. There were no "catchers" so she hit the ground hard. She jumped up and asked for prayer again. The last time she stood, I just moved on and left her standing in line. The next day, I went to the pastor's house for lunch. When we pulled up to his house, this woman (I did not know she was a witch doctor or that she was an agent of the devil came to the car and requested a few minutes to talk to me. I agreed, and she began to tell me her story.

She explained that whenever men and women of God came to the city of Lomé, that she attends and casts spells on the people. She explained that it was her who had struck my translators with dumbness. She also explained that she tried to place a spell on me but that it bounced back and hit her. She came forward to have hands laid upon her as this was the way of making contact to impart her curse but the power of God in me was stronger than the force of Satan in her life.

She received Jesus as Lord, and I cast a legion of demons out of her right on the street outside the pastor's house. The point that I am trying to make is there are times that you have to make a bold stand like I did when I shouted. This bold shout became the vehicle for the anointing to break the yoke that they were trying to exert in my meeting. The greater One, who lives in me, was able to manifest His power. The gates of hades could not prevail.

There are times that our lives come under direct attack. When we sense evil manifesting in our environment or in our lives, we must make a bold stand and rebuke the spirit to depart. This is spiritual warfare. When you resist the devil and his cohorts, they will flee from you.

"Therefore submit to God. Resist the devil and he will flee from you" (James 4:7).

We live in this world, but we are not of this world. As carriers of the presence of God, we are going to be in contact with these evil forces that are working to slow us down, stop the Church and hinder our lives. We are engaged in a war. Thankfully, we are not alone; we have God on our side. Not only on our side but on our inside. Greater is He that is in us than he that is in the world (1 John 4:4). "If God be for us, who can be against us" (Romans 8:31). We must be bold in spiritual warfare; we must make a stand and fight the good fight of faith.

Chapter 8

Bold Giving

Within days of being saved, I had a dream that was crystal clear. I heard the voice of God, "Leon, you will never out-give me!" It was apparent that God wanted me to become a generous giver. Since receiving that dream until today, I have willingly given my tithes and offerings every month. I have given in season and out of season. I have worshiped God with my offerings and made this a priority. This has never been done as a burden or under duress, but I have given cheerfully and generously. As a result of my obedience, and the grace of God, I live in the provision and care of God.

There is no way that anyone can out-give God because He so loved us that He gave Jesus to die for us. (John 3:16) God sent Jesus to take our place in suffering, and He did for us what we could not do for ourselves. Jesus took what we deserved so that we may have access to God's provision.

The Apostle Paul summarizes this:

Now thanks be to God for His Gift, [precious] beyond telling [His indescribable, inexpressible, free Gift]! (2 Corinthians 9:15 AMP)

I do not want you to have any confusion concerning my motive in addressing this subject. I realize that the number one hatred people have concerning preachers is that they think we only speak about money. Possibly there is a small percentage of preachers who attempt to extort gullible followers. However, statistically most pastors don't address this subject. The reason a high percentage of pastors avoid discussing finances is that they lack boldness. Perhaps, some are more afraid of what people think than what God thinks. The Bible is clear that people perish for a lack of knowledge. Members of the church are living in ignorance concerning God's plan for their lives financially because they are untaught. People are living in debt, lack, and in disobedience, because their pastors are afraid to teach with conviction what the Bible says about giving and receiving. If a pastor doesn't teach on God's plan for Christians to give, then they may be pleasing the people, but in the process, they have compromised God's Word. They may make the people feel happy through excluding this in their sermon collection, but how does God feel about the matter? Paul made this statement, and I think every Christian leader should take note and do the same:

For I have not shunned to declare to you the whole counsel of God. (Acts 20:27)

They should uncompromisingly give instruction from the whole counsel of God's Word. No Biblical truth should be suppressed for fear of being misunderstood and misjudged by the people. What about the account that we as teachers will with certainty give before Almighty God? The reason I teach about giving is that I will not neglect what is included in Scripture. If the hearers of the Word obey and bring their offerings, they will receive their provision. I know that if the people give their offerings with the right heart motive that they will live in the constant provision of God.

I teach on Biblical stewardship because faith comes by hearing and hearing by the Word of God. People should know what God's Word says and be able to sow in faith and then they will reap the benefits of God's abundance. It takes faith to sow finances. If the giver does not lose heart, there is a due harvest when they will reap the harvest. God is watching over His Word to perform it for their lives.

Teaching on giving is important because God's people are going to be the primary way that He will finance the work of ministry. The Red Cross will not advance the Gospel only Christians will pay for this to take place. The Mafia will not finance soul winning or world missions only Christians will care enough to invest into the harvest of souls. Secular businesses won't pay for the construction of Bible Schools or Churches only generous and faithful Christians will pay for the work of God. The only ones who will finance the advance of the Kingdom are the citizens of the Kingdom.

Remember, this subject is not just about giving; it is about giving and receiving. We cannot out-give God. He is the Provider, and He is going to give back pressed down, shaken together and running over. When we give we are in fact taking the seed God has already given us and as we boldly give, we can then watch Him cause a harvest. God gives each believer something to sow; when they do this, then God will bring the increase. God gives us seed to sow and then He gives an increase.

And God is able to make all grace abound toward you, that you, always having all sufficiency in all things, may have an abundance for every good work. (2 Corinthians 9:8)

Bold givers will be the recipients of the constant supply of resource that will come into their lives for the funding of the work of God. There will be more than enough to eat, live and then more than enough to finance the last day's ministry.

Generosity and Boldness

What I have noticed in the USA, (I can't speak for other nations), is that people just don't give as they did say 20 or 30 years ago. Now I realize that this is a broad statement, so perhaps I am not accurate. You can decide if I am accurate or not. I would say when the economy took a plunge with the collapse of the housing market in the USA that was when the way Christians gave started to change. I also assume that negative publicity has exposed outrageous salaries and expenses for certain renowned preachers, and this communication, has caused people mistrust the ministry and in turn they give less. Remember, this is a broad stroke, and I am generalizing. I have met some of the most generous people who give regardless of what's happening in the economics or the USA or the world.

1.   Bold giving is not determined by the economic climate, but it is in spite of the economy.

2.   Bold giving is not determined by how much or how little money you have, but is based on the size of your vision and faith.

3.   Bold giving is not determined by the manipulation of a preacher who can persuade you to write a check for more than you had planned, but rather on your ability to hear God, and do what he says.

I think that generosity and boldness go hand in hand; It takes boldness to write a generous check. It takes boldness to give generously with the guarantee that the seed you have sown will in due season produce for you a harvest.

I was preaching in a village in Togo where just two days before I had led about 200 people to Christ in the middle of the market. I had to leave these new converts to go to another village a few hours away, and so I told the people that I would return. There was no church in this village, and so I had promised that I would return to plant one. As promised, I returned and began to preach to an even larger crowd than my first duration in this village. The word spread about the miracles and the people wanted salvation. While I was preaching a man in torn shorts and a well-worn tee shirt stood close to my side listening to the Word of God. Wherever I walked in the village this man in torn clothes followed me like my shadow. I took a short rest and this same man in the torn and well-worn clothing approached me. This is exactly what he said to me, "Two days ago I was in the market, I heard you preach and gave my heart to the Lord and I was saved." I said, "Praise the Lord!" He then went on, "I am standing there listening to you preach and the Lord spoke to me, (Remember, this is a two day old Christian who doesn't own a Bible and no church in the community), "The Lord told me to give you my inheritance, a plot of land to build the church." This new brother and I ran about a half mile to view the land, then we ran to meet his uncle who was the Chief of the village. I had to then run back to the car that was waiting as I had a six-hour drive to get back to the City for an outreach meeting that evening. This man, a two day old Christian, gave his entire inheritance for a church to be built…now that's bold giving!

Bold giving cannot be limited to money. We give ourselves in our entirety to God. We hold nothing back; no reserves in case this new thing doesn't work. Elisha boldly gave his oxen, his plow, his fields, his very life to serve Elijah. That was pretty bold! He held nothing back. No reserves, no retreat possibility. He gave everything away. (1 Kings 19:19-21)

You will see this same kind of generosity displayed when the Church gave to the suffering Church in Jerusalem.

They gave boldly and generously to their brothers who were in an intense famine. Before they gave their finances they first gave themselves to the Lord.

Moreover, brethren, we make known to you the grace of God bestowed on the churches of Macedonia: that in a great trial of affliction the abundance of their joy and their deep poverty abounded in the riches of their liberality. For I bear witness that according to their ability, yes, and beyond their ability, they were freely willing, imploring us with much urgency that we would receive the gift and the fellowship of the ministering to the saints. And not only as we had hoped, but they first gave themselves to the Lord, and then to us by the will of God. (2 Corinthians 8:1-5)

Like I said, this is actually about giving yourself to God first; then it's about giving your life to others. (1 John 3:16; John 15;13) This is true sacrificial living; when we are willing to go out of our way for someone else. When we give to serve and help someone else, we are in reality doing it unto the Lord. There are two areas where we express our bold and generous giving:

1. Giving ourselves to serve in the church; this includes helping the family of God whenever it is our ability.

2. Giving of ourselves to serve and compassionately touch or reach the lost.

Barnabas was bold when he gave generously

And Joses, who was also named Barnabas by the apostles (which is translated Son of Encouragement), a Levite of the country of Cyprus, having land, sold it, and brought the money and laid it at the apostles' feet. (Acts 4:36-37)

The early Christians began to express care for one another through their giving. This was not legalism but love in action; no one was forced to give and express care for one another in this way. Neither was this an offering that was manipulated by the Apostles; it does not state that the Apostles requested this generosity. On the contrary, it would seem that it was a rather spontaneous eruption of generosity and boldness. (Acts 2:44-45; 4:32-35) While this was taking place, Barnabas went and got the title to his land, sold it and brought the full amount and laid it at the Apostle's feet as an act of worship to God and expressing love for the saints who were in need. This bold act of generosity sparked a wave of giving from others. When Barnabas gave his land as an offering, it was sacrificial giving, because that land was his retirement, his pension, and would be his security. This was a significant offering; probably something he could afford to do, but he did it because he loved God and the Church.

The Woman who Loved Much

Then one of the Pharisees asked Him to eat with him. And He went to the Pharisee's house, and sat down to eat. And behold, a woman in the city who was a sinner, when she knew that Jesus sat at the table in the Pharisee's house, brought an alabaster flask of fragrant oil, and stood at His feet behind Him weeping; and she began to wash His feet with her tears, and wiped them with the hair of her head; and she kissed His feet and anointed them with the fragrant oil. (Luke 7:36-38)

Then He turned to the woman and said to Simon, "Do you see this woman? I entered your house; you gave Me no water for My feet, but she has washed My feet with her tears and wiped them with the hair of her head. You gave Me no kiss, but this woman has not ceased to kiss My feet since the time I came in. You did not anoint My head with oil, but this woman has anointed My feet with fragrant oil. Therefore, I say to you, her sins, which are many, are forgiven, for she loved much. But to whom little is forgiven, the same loves little." (Luke 7:44-47)

This is a great Bible account of appreciation and generosity, but it also demonstrates passion and boldness. It must have been a pretty emotional moment. Can you imagine what went on in the minds of the people when she came into the room with such brokenness, intensity, and boldness kissed the feet of Jesus? With tears streaming down her face onto the feet of Jesus; she then dried His saturated feet with her hair. She then poured costly anointing oil on Him. This was a bold move; entering into the Pharisees home, passing by all the people outside waiting for Jesus to exit. Going into the house passing all the people pressed into the home; realizing everyone probably knew of her and her sinning lifestyle. She eventually fell at the feet of Jesus in an outburst of unbridled emotion. What an amazing scene? She was bold, generous and deeply appreciative for God's mercy displayed through Jesus.

David's Mighty Men

Then three of the thirty chief men went down at harvest time and came to David at the cave of Adullam. And the troop of Philistines encamped in the Valley of Rephaim. David was then in the stronghold, and the garrison of the Philistines was then in Bethlehem. And David said with longing, "Oh, that someone would give me a drink of the water from the well of Bethlehem, which is by the gate!" So the three mighty men broke through the camp of the Philistines, drew water from the well of Bethlehem that was by the gate, and took it and brought it to David. Nevertheless, he would not drink it, but poured it out to the LORD. And he said, "Far be it from me, O LORD, that I should do this! Is this not the blood of the men who went in jeopardy of their lives?" Therefore, he would not drink it. These things were done by the three mighty men. (2 Samuel 23:13-17)

This is an incredible story of honor, love, loyalty, heroism, generosity and boldness. I could teach from this portion of Scripture for hours expounding the many imbedded truths displayed in these verses of Scripture. These were amazing men! As I read this story, I also love the heart of David as he genuinely values these valiant men and interprets what they did for him as an act of worship to God. These three soldiers heard David's desire to drink from that well in Bethlehem. The water must have been cold, clear and sweet. He was not hinting to his men but just talking about his thirst and desire for some quality water. The men spontaneously seized an opportunity to make a difference in their leader's life through an act of bold generosity. Some people would think that they were foolish; I don't! I think they were awesome brave soldiers who cared deeply for their King in the making. They obviously counted the cost, knowing that they would penetrate deeply into enemy territory and after their evaluation decided that the risk was nothing in comparison to the reward (Their only reward was to see the smile on David's face as he drank the quality water that he desired) That's bold giving at its best!

She gave her Last Meal!

There are times that we purpose in our heart what we want to give as an offering to God. (2 Corinthians 9:7) Then there are times when God tells us what we should give. To obey is better than sacrifice, and when God tell us to give it is NEVER for our loss but for our gain. God will not ask us to give something away unless He has a plan to supply for us. He will use our gift as a seed, and then He will provide for us a harvest of much more than we originally gave. This was the case with the widow in the famine.

Then the word of the LORD came to him, saying "Arise, go to Zarephath, which belongs to Sidon, and dwell there. See, I have commanded a widow there to provide for you." So he arose and went to Zarephath. And when he came to the gate of the city, indeed a widow was there gathering sticks. And he called to her and said, "Please bring me a little water in a cup, that I may drink." And as she was going to get it, he called to her and said, "Please bring me a morsel of bread in your hand." So she said, "As the LORD your God lives, I do not have bread, only a handful of flour in a bin, and a little oil in a jar; and see, I am gathering a couple of sticks that I may go in and prepare it for myself and my son, that we may eat it, and die." And Elijah said to her, "Do not fear; go and do as you have said, but make me a small cake from it first, and bring it to me; and afterward make some for yourself and your son. For thus says the LORD God of Israel: 'The bin of flour shall not be used up, nor shall the jar of oil run dry, until the day the LORD sends rain on the earth.' " So she went away and did according to the word of Elijah; and she and he and her household ate for many days. The bin of flour was not used up, nor did the jar of oil run dry, according to the word of the LORD which He spoke by Elijah. (1 Kings 17:8-16)

God had supplied food for Elijah by speaking to ravens, and they would bring him some of their food. The birds obeyed God. God then told Elijah to travel to Zarephath as he had a new source of provision for him. In the interim God had also spoken to a widow to provide for the prophet Elijah from her last meal. The Widow heard the voice of God to feed the Elijah. She eventually obeyed the voice of God, but this was through the involvement of the prophet when he asked her to bake him some bread. Her feeding the prophet FIRST, was a step of faith, in unsuitable circumstances but it would trigger a miracle for her life.

It was not an ideal time for her to give but as she obeyed God's instructions and took a bold step and the provision for her miracle was released into her account. Had she not obeyed the word of the prophet, the widow and her family would have died of starvation. The miracle of God's provision for her came about as a direct result of giving. In spite of her poverty and need, she boldly obeyed and gave to the prophet. The key to her breakthrough was her bold giving when lack was screaming at her, "Don't do it!"

Be bold in your giving!

I want to address a rather sensitive issue but feel that in the light of this subject it will be appropriate. When it comes to Kingdom giving, I find some Christians give the least amount possible, like one dollar. This would be ok if they were like the widow with her last coin, but this is not what I am addressing.

I will give you an example:

People attend special meetings, and they take a break for lunch, and everyone goes off to their favorite place to eat. Some buy a Big Mac, others go to a restaurant and order a soup and salad, and some people will even buy a steak, salad, and drink. Their bill for lunch comes in at around $8 to $15 plus a 15% tip. They go back to the conference and at the end of 6 hours of ministry the church will receive a special offering, and most the people will give $1, others a $5 offering and handful of others may even give $10. You have to hear me – it's not the amount, it's the priority. They will spend $8 to $15 plus tip on lunch and then give $1 in the offering. Something is wrong! I know many evangelists, missionaries and traveling Apostles that struggle to survive. They could make more money flipping burgers. These are qualified and anointed preachers. They have years of ministry experience, and everyone wants a word and a touch from God through their lives, but the recipients won't be bold in their giving. Some people give the lowest denomination possible. They will spend more on a cup of coffee at a 711 (not even talking about a fancy latte at Starbucks) than the offering. They pay $2.00 or more for a coffee and then put $1 in the offering. There is no sacrifice or honor in their giving; there is no sincere worship. They give what is convenient! This same principle can apply to offerings for missions, special projects, or as used in this illustration of a guest ministry.

Fear prevents people from giving sacrificially. They will spend generously on their lunch, their hobbies and interests, but they give stingingly when it comes to the work of God.

Bold Giving

It's strange how money will reveal the heart. "For where your treasure is, there is your heart also." (Matthew 6:21) The priorities of your heart and your spending/giving are inseparable. It's the same as the things that you talk about most are the real things taking place or being revealed from your heart. What you do or don't do is what you really believe in. Our giving, our talking and the things that we do are what is in the heart. If the priorities of eternity are in your heart, then the way you give will be the evidence.

To win this generation it will take a lot of funding. There are organizations that are gaining momentum with their agendas. They are heavily financed, and they are using their income to change the conscience of a nation. They are promoting their message, and they are having famous people underwrite them. At the same time, the Church is being muted from communicating our message because the finances are not there to get the word out. The Church is going to need bold giving! We need to be like the early church, when the people began to spontaneously give. There was a spontaneous eruption of bold giving. The people were not manipulated or coerced, but they simply gave from their heart. The early believers gave to God as a people of vision. Bold giving is found in people who are saved, in first love with Jesus, and who have vision.

Bold givers and bold preachers will be responsible for the harvest. Not just bold preaching, but a teamwork of bold

141

BOLD

praying, bold leadership, bold preaching, and bold giving and we can win this generation.

Chapter 9

Bold Leadership

To paraphrase a tagline from Star Trek, "Leaders must boldly go where no one has gone before"—or at least, they will have to step aside from the masses, and take God's people to where God wants them to go.

Leaders, or better said, spiritual leaders, are men and women who have been promoted by God to care, train, build, protect, and serve God's people. They are not like leaders in business, sports, the military or other professions—they are spiritual leaders anointed and raised by God to do His will. They are not merely busy, creative, or industrious—though none of these characteristics are wrong but they have to be operating in the right order.

The right order is for God's will to be done at all costs. Spiritual leaders are about the business of God. They are not competitive; they are not on an ego trip; they are not doing their own thing, rather, they are busy doing all that God has called them to accomplish.

This kind of boldness that leaders must possess is a direct deposit from God into their hearts. The bold presence of God operating in the heart makes a leader secure and confident. Bold leaders will inspire change, progress, and advance the Gospel. Through bold leadership, the Church will see the release of spiritual impetus and a big vision will be fulfilled. Bold leaders will inspire God's people to be their best for the glory of God.

God made David Bold

"In the day when I cried out, You answered me, And made me bold with strength in my soul" (Psalm 138:3).

This Psalm is attributed to David and was penned when he sought God for boldness because of the attack against his kingdom and his leadership. The surrounding nations, the Jebusites, Philistines, and Moabites were targeting his leadership because they knew if they could divide the kingdom, they would gain supremacy. They knew if David was weakened, they would defeat Israel. David prayed, God heard and gave him deliverance—he was able to defeat his enemies.

David was a great biblical example of bold leadership. As the shepherd boy, the giant killer, and the king, he exuded boldness. His life was one of poise, dignity, and courage. David was bold in the face of danger when he protected his father's flock from the lion and the bear (1 Samuel 17:36). Again, he operated in boldness in making himself available to King Saul to destroy the giant, Goliath (1 Samuel 17). I think David was willing to take on the entire army of the Philistines if he had to, but he was going to deliver Israel. I also imagine that David wanted to kill Goliath and the other four giants in the land. He was not inspired by the promises of tax-free living or marriage into Saul's family, but he was motivated by his passion for God.

David was not an arrogant leader—he was bold. If David was arrogant and self-promoting, he would have killed Saul when he had the opportunity. Rather, David spared King Saul, and he patiently waited for God's timing and promotion. Being bold is not self-promoting. He had a deep sense of honor for God to be exalted in all the nation of Israel.

Peter and John were Bold Leaders

"Now when they saw the boldness of Peter and John, and perceived that they were uneducated and untrained men, they marveled. And they realized that they had been with Jesus" (Acts 4:13).

When a person "hangs with Jesus," there is an impartation from Him to that person's spirit. Something of the resident boldness of God that was in Jesus was placed into his or her life. Even the religious leaders of the day had to acknowledge that Peter and John possessed a calm and boldness that was unexpected. However, they also recognized these qualities as the evidence of being with Jesus. As a leader, we need to possess spiritual boldness that flows from fellowship with Jesus. Ordinary disciples, simple followers were transformed into bold leaders when they got close to Jesus. Leaders need to spend time in the presence of the boldest of all leaders and receive divine impartation into their spirits.

BOLD

Leadership requires boldness

When God calls and promotes a person into leadership, it is an honorable position. However, being a leader who represents God is not an easy task. Ask Moses! As a leader, we will face some serious confrontations and challenges:

1. Being a leader in the Kingdom is not for the faint of heart but the bold.

2. The legions of darkness will resist our leadership and vision. They will seek to thwart our every God-given assignment.

3. The world will despise passionate Christian leaders. The passionate leader carries a God-boldness that somehow offends people who are in darkness.

4. Carnal Christians will at times be used by the devil to slow down and hinder the ministry of a leader from being effective. These carnal Christians may even be more critical of a leader than sinners. The spiritual leader must be bold not to be intimidated by these critics.

5. Jealous Christian leaders will be envious of the anointing on a spiritual leader; some may even turn against their peers and seek to undermine their influence in the Christian community. It takes boldness to stand strong in the face of unfair and hostile critics especially from within

the ranks of the Christian community. I have never been bothered by critics who are not in the body of Christ, but when a brother criticizes, that hurts! We need to be bold that we don't become wounded and feel inadequate.

6. Leaders need to be bold because they will face rejection, unfair criticism, and harsh judgments will be leveled against them.

Being Bold as a Leaders is not Enough

- You must be a servant in attitude

- You must be humble

- You must be sacrificial

- You must be spiritual

- You must be loving

- You must be compassionate

If you are a visionary leader, your workload will be great, and the immediate rewards lacking (the rewards will mostly be out of this world). These leaders must live from the baseline of the fellowship of the Spirit and the inspiration that He gives. The path of the leader is often lonely (even though your life is surrounded by people). The ever increasing busyness of your leadership roles will catch up with you. To survive, let alone succeed, will require boldness.

BOLD

Boldness Defined:

Courageous, confident, and fearless; ready to take risks. Showing or requiring courage: a bold plan (Dictionary.com)

I want to describe in a concise way what "bold leadership" looks like and remove any misconceptions that could exist in understanding how it looks. When we say that someone has "bold leadership," you may imagine that this person possesses a charismatic personality. You may perceive that a bold leader is a person who wants to succeed at all costs. You may also be thinking that this kind of leader will always obtain their every desire and goal. These leaders don't take no for an answer, and they always get what they want even if they manipulate others (including their followers) to do what is needed to reach their goals. This perception of a bold leader is far-removed from the spiritual leader portrayed in the New Testament. Certainly, I don't want to describe the bold leader as a person who is arrogant, win-at-any-cost, or abusive towards their followers.

Jim Rohn, a business person, defines bold leadership:

"The challenge of leadership is to be strong, but not rude; be kind, but not weak; be bold, but not bully; be thoughtful, but not lazy; be humble, but not timid; be proud, but not arrogant; have humor, but without folly."

Bold Leadership

Boldness should not be confused with being arrogant

"Now I, Paul, myself am pleading with you by the meekness and gentleness of Christ--who in presence am lowly among you, but being absent am bold toward you" (2 Corinthians 10:1).

Like the Apostle Paul, spiritual leaders are to be bold but not arrogant. They are to operate with a Christlike attitude while being bold at the same time; being bold should not be in conflict with being humble. The combination of being bold and being humble is best seen in Jesus. When Jesus drove out the money-changers from the temple, He was bold. He had the character to be bold in the face of unrighteous charlatans, yet, He held the little children in His arms and blessed them. Bold leaders may exert confidence and assurance but running parallel to these characteristics must be a heart of sensitivity to even their weakest follower. Bold leaders can take huge strides of vision, but they move at the pace of their followers. They are bold in attitude, yet, tender at the same time.

The spiritual leader cannot be subject to the fear of man. They cannot be dominated by the pursuit of prominence or riches. Spiritual leaders are servants of God and their only pursuit is to do the will of God. These leaders will work with the great and small, the weak and the strong. They will work with business people, government officials, and other leaders. These leaders will also work with the poor, the uneducated, and the rejects of society (Christ came to seek and to save the lost).

To be effective, these leaders will have to know how to negotiate with a sense of diplomacy and tact with all men. They should as much as possible always seek to win people to the Lord and to inspire those impacted by their ministries to be engaged in the work of expanding His Kingdom.

John the Baptist was a bold leader, but his unflinching standard of purity would cost him his head on a platter. He was not an arrogant man, but he was intensely bold. Sometimes, a bold leader will lose his head in the process of doing the right thing but that's the price of being uncompromisingly secure in his or her calling. There is a fine line between leading with confidence, and being perceived by your critics as being arrogant. Bold leaders have to do what is in their hearts and allow God to be the Judge. There is no way the leaders can defend themselves; they have to trust that vindication will come from God.

Jesus entered into the temple with zeal and with divine authority. He cleansed the temple of unrighteous business that was being conducted in the house of prayer. His boldness and righteous indignation could be interpreted as uncontrolled rage by His critics. Again, what He did as a bold leader was not understood by His critics. Anyone who will make this kind of bold stand will be misunderstood, criticized, and despised, but they just have to take the abuse and get on with their lives and ministry. Welcome to bold leadership!

All Christians need boldness, but it is an absolute essential for spiritual leaders to operate in boldness.

Leadership requires boldness—strength, courage, and confidence. The requirement of courage was stressed in the encounter Joshua had with the Angel of the Lord before leading the people into the Promised Land. The instruction that he was given from the Lord is as applicable to us as leaders today as it was to him approximately four thousand years ago. Three times, he was told to possess the attitude of courage or boldness. This attitude of courage would be essential to gain the advantage over the enemies of Israel and to possess the land. Joshua would also need courage because he was going to lead a tough and complex people.

> Be strong and of good courage, for to this people you shall divide as an inheritance the land which I swore to their fathers to give them. Only be strong and very courageous, that you may observe to do according to all the law which Moses My servant commanded you; do not turn from it to the right hand or to the left, that you may prosper wherever you go. This Book of the Law shall not depart from your mouth, but you shall meditate in it day and night, that you may observe to do according to all that is written in it. For then you will make your way prosperous, and then you will have good success. Have I not commanded you? Be

strong and of good courage; do not be afraid, nor be dismayed, for the LORD your God is with you wherever you go." (Joshua 1:6-9)

"But even after we had suffered before and were spitefully treated at Philippi, as you know, we were bold in our God to speak to you the gospel of God in much conflict" (1 Thessalonians 2:2).

Every person who embraces the call of God to function as a leader will have to face enemies. We will face multiple, impossible situations; being opposed by people and demons will become a way of life. As leaders, we must be armed with courage and boldness. David's defeat of the giant became a launchpad for his leadership. The battles you face will, in the same way, become the launchpad for your ministry to be received and celebrated by those who will follow you.

We don't have to make bold claims to be bold!

There is a difference between making bold claims and actually being bold. Peter made bold claims that he would be loyal to Jesus but under pressure, he ended up denying even knowing the Lord. To Peter's defense, after the resurrection and the subsequent Pentecost experience, he became a fearless leader. Leaders don't have to affirm their loyalty, courage or commitment— they simply have to do it.

Why should leaders be bold in the Lord?

Leaders will mostly face unfair criticism. Therefore, they must be bold. There are times a leader will say or do things that deserve some criticism.

"Then Paul and Barnabas grew bold and said, 'It was necessary that the word of God should be spoken to you first; but since you reject it, and judge yourselves unworthy of everlasting life, behold, we turn to the Gentiles" (Acts 13:46).

1. Leaders must be bold as they will need to make tough decisions.

2. Every decision will meet with acceptance as well as resistance.

Part and parcel of leadership responsibility is making decisions—sometimes, tough decisions. When leaders make decisions, their followers react differently:

There are those who accept and approve our decisions.

1. These people are normally supportive and encouraging.

2. They don't mind the process of change as they are flexible, and they can go with the flow.

There are those who disapprove and reject the decisions of their leaders.

1. These people can be resistors of change; stuck in a rut mentality.

2. They can also be arrogant and because they were not included in the decision-making process, they automatically reject the decisions and directions.

3. They can also be smart and see things that the leaders didn't take into account.

There are those who simply go with the flow; they are not enthusiastic or negative. These are the indifferent followers. If enough pressure (negative or positive) is placed on them, they may drift to one opinion. My experience is these followers are motivated by loyalties (family or friendship) rather than personal convictions.

Leaders are visionaries. Fulfilling vision (big!) takes bold leadership and bold decision making.

The reality is, without a vision you not only perish but also, you are not a leader. It is a contradiction of reality—a leader possesses vision or better said, "Vision possesses a leader." Leaders are going somewhere, (that somewhere is called vision) and in the process of reaching their vision, they take people with them.

These followers journeying with them are not a means to an end. They are not disposable, but they are precious to God; trophies of His grace and love. Godly leaders are always given visions that are bigger than themselves. These visions will stretch them in their skills, abilities, and their faith. Typically, for a leader to fulfill a God-given mandate, it will take a few miracles. Leaders will have to be bold in their decision-making as well as in their ability to execute the vision. A few biblical classics that support this:

God assigned Moses the task to lead the Israelites out of Egypt. This mandate was far bigger than Moses; he would be stretched in every area of his life and leadership to fulfill it. Besides Moses' ability, God would have to work some miracles to bring this huge vision into existence.

God gave Noah a mission that would take over a hundred and twenty years to complete. The spiritual environment was hostile, and Noah would have to go into realms unvisited by man. He truly went where no one had been before.

All spiritual leadership requires bold leadership. There will always be "Impossible" written over the entrance. Or if not "Impossible,"— "Entrance Forbidden!" It takes faith, patience, and boldness to embrace a God-given assignment.

Leaders set standards for conduct and membership within their ranks or organizations. To enforce standards that are biblical will mean bringing correction and direction. Leaders have to be firm to confront (in a loving way), this requires being bold.

"Now I, Paul, myself am pleading with you by the meekness and gentleness of Christ--who in presence am lowly among you, but being absent am bold toward you" (2 Corinthians 10:1).

In this verse, we see gentleness and boldness wrapped together. A balanced leader can be bold while remaining gentle. Mature leaders are not easily irritated at the stuff that goes wrong or when plans don't go the way they expected. They don't react with irritation, but they respond with poise and grace. However, a balanced leader is not afraid to confront behaviors or attitudes that disrupt the unity of the Spirit. They will confront rebellion, division, and anyone who seeks to devour the flock. They understand the difference between protecting the flock and beating a wolf.

Leaders have to be bold enough to confront their friends and trusted staff. I have seen leaders lack the boldness to confront and put into place their staff or leaders and the "problem" escalated. In my life and ministry, I have procrastinated confronting people to the point that the issue blew up in my face. To be frank, I lacked the courage to do what I should have done. My delays in dealing with certain issues have cost me more than the losses upfront. I have learned through the school of hard knocks that it's better to lose some people earlier than have the leaven of division rob the leaders upfront rather than in the messiness of the leadership structure.

Leaders will exert influence into the "spiritual climate" (like Elijah on Mt. Carmel) and stand in faith when it appears that very little is apparently taking place; this is why leaders require boldness.

Leaders carve a trail (they are Trail Blazers). They go where no one has gone before, or at least, where only a few have ventured; this journey requires boldness.